W0036595

► Palliative Care and End-of-Life Decisions

DOI: 10.1057/9781137377395

Also by George P. Smith

LAW AND BIOETHICS: INTERSECTIONS ALONG THE MORTAL COIL

DISTRIBUTIVE JUSTICE AND THE NEW MEDICINE

THE CHRISTIAN RELIGION AND BIOTECHNOLOGY: A Search for Principled Decision-making

HUMAN RIGHTS AND BIOMEDICINE

FAMILY VALUES AND THE NEW SOCIETY

LEGAL AND HEALTHCARE ETHICS FOR THE ELDERLY

BIOETHICS AND THE LAW: Medical, Socio-legal, and Philosophical Directions for a Brave New World

THE NEW BIOLOGY: Law, Ethics, and Biotechnology

FINAL CHOICES: Autonomy in Health Care Decisions

MEDICAL-LEGAL ASPECTS OF CRYONICS

ETHICAL, LEGAL, AND SOCIAL CHALLENGES TO A BRAVE NEW WORLD

GENETICS, ETHICS, AND THE LAW

DOI: 10.1057/9781137377395

palgrave▸pivot

Palliative Care and End-of-Life Decisions

George P. Smith, II
The Catholic University of America, USA

palgrave
macmillan

DOI: 10.1057/9781137377395

PALLIATIVE CARE AND END-OF-LIFE DECISIONS
Copyright © George P. Smith, 2013.

All rights reserved.

First published in 2013 by
PALGRAVE MACMILLAN®
in the United States—a division of St. Martin's Press LLC,
175 Fifth Avenue, New York, NY 10010.

Where this book is distributed in the UK, Europe and the rest of the world, this is by Palgrave Macmillan, a division of Macmillan Publishers Limited, registered in England, company number 785998, of Houndmills, Basingstoke, Hampshire RG21 6XS.

Palgrave Macmillan is the global academic imprint of the above companies and has companies and representatives throughout the world.

Palgrave® and Macmillan® are registered trademarks in the United States, the United Kingdom, Europe and other countries.

ISBN: 978-1-137-37737-1 EPUB
ISBN: 978-1-137-37739-5 PDF
ISBN: 978-1-137-37915-3 Hardback

Library of Congress Cataloging-in-Publication Data is available from the Library of Congress.

A catalogue record of the book is available from the British Library.

First edition: 2013

www.palgrave.com/pivot

DOI: 10.1057/9781137377395

For

*John H. Lynch, M.D., Anatoly Dritschillo, M.D., Sean P.
Collins, M.D., and Loretta S. "Coach" Hamilton, R.N., with
immeasurable gratitude for the superior health care that
I have received from them at the Georgetown University
Medical Center*

and to the memory of

*Myles N. Brand, Harold A. Buetow, Mildred E. Hipskind,
Martha J. Jones, Ruth A. Jones, Colleen K. Pauwels, Edmund
D. Pellegrino, Harry Pratter, Herman B Wells, David G. T.
Williams and George G. Winterton*

DOI: 10.1057/9781137377395

Contents

DOI: 10.1057/9781137377395

Preface

Since the beginning of the hospice movement in 1967, "total pain management" has been the declared goal of hospice care. Palliating the whole person's physical, psycho-social, and spiritual states or conditions are central to managing pain which induces suffering. At the end stage of life, an inextricable component of an ethics of adjusted care requires recognition of a fundamental right to avoid cruel and unusual suffering from terminal illness. This book urges wider consideration and use of terminal sedation, or sedation until death, as efficacious palliative treatment and as a reasonable medical procedure in order to safeguard a "right" to a dignified death.

Absent the recognition of a constitutional right or, for that matter, liberty interest in dying with dignity, the best position would be to but accept and recognize the common law right to resist physical intrusion as the corner stone for refusing treatment—thereby embracing a more compassionate and enlightened ethic of understanding in managing end-of-life issues.

If a human right to avoid refractory pain of whatever nature in end-stage illness is, however, established by the state, a co-ordinate responsibility must be assumed by health care providers to make medical judgments consistent with preserving the best interests of a patient's quality of life by alleviating suffering. The principle of medical futility is the preferred construct for implementing this professional responsibility.

Rather than continuing to be mired in the vexatious quagmire of the doctrine of double effect—all in an effort to "test" whether end-stage decisions by health care providers are licit or illicit—a relatively simple test of proportionality, or cost-benefit analysis, is proffered.

Imbedded, necessarily, in this equation is the humane virtue of compassion, charity, mercy or *agape*.

Assertions of state interest to safeguard public morality by restricting intimate associational freedoms to accelerate death in a terminal illness are suspicious if, indeed, not invalid. No individual should be forced to live when, in a futile medical condition, he or she is suffering from intractable somatic and/or non-somatic existential pain.

The major bioethical issues and their clinical applications presented in this book have been tested in the "market place of ideas" in seven major lectures that I have delivered: "Strategizing the End-Game: Palliative Medicine and the Law," at the Faculty of Law, University of Oxford, England, 2012; "Seeking an Easeful Death: Permutations within a Penumbra," at The Rothermere Institute, University of Oxford, England, 2012; "Managing End-of-Life Care: Medico-Legal, Social, Ethical, and Philosophical Challenges," The Myles N. Brand Lecture, Center for Law, Ethics, and Applied Research in Health Information, at the Indiana University School of Law, 2011; "Bioethics and Human Rights: Toward a New Constitutionalism," a George G. Winterton Memorial Lecture, at the University of Sydney, Australia, 2010; "The Quality of Mercy and Common Dignity: Safeguarding The Last Right," a University Lecture at The University of St. Andrews, Scotland, 2007; and "Of Panjandrums, Pooh-Bahs, Parvenus, and Prophets: Law, Religion, and Medical Science," The Michael D. Kirby Lecture, Macquarie University Faculty of Law, Australia, 2005.

This book is drawn also from my article, *Refractory Pain, Existential Suffering, and Palliative Care: Releasing an Unbearable Lightness of Being,* 20 CORNELL JOURNAL OF LAW AND PUBLIC POLICY 469–532 (2011) and completes development of my Bioethics—Health Care epistemology that I posited initially with the publication of *All's Well That Ends Well: Toward a Policy of Assisted Rational Suicide or Merely Enlightened Self-Determination?*, 22 U.C. DAVIS L. REV. 275–419 (1989).

DOI: 10.1057/9781137377395

1

Broadening the Boundaries of Palliative Medicine

Abstract: *Acknowledging the great promise of palliative care management for assuring that the end-of-life becomes a more compassionate experience, this book's bold thesis advocates the liberal use of sedative medications to relieve refractory distress by the reduction in patient consciousness. Accordingly, palliative sedation therapy must be seen as proper medical treatment and consistent with sound principles of adjusted care which, in turn, should be the standard for all hospice medicine. When a diagnosis and prognosis present the patient as suffering a futile medical condition, and where patient consent or surrogate approval is obtained, compassion directs palliative (or terminal) sedation be offered as efficacious treatment to alleviate intractable physical and existential suffering.*

George P. Smith. *Palliative Care and End-of-Life Decisions.* New York: Palgrave Macmillan, 2013. DOI: 10.1057/9781137377395.

Over the next 30 years, the projected population of seniors in the United States will more than double—rising from 34 million in 1997 to, by 2030, over 69 million.[1] By that time, one out of five Americans will have attained the age of 65 or older.[2] For baby boomers, one in nine may expect to reach the age of 90; and by the year 2040, those Americans over the age of 85 will have reached nearly four times that of those in 2003.[3] The potential use of both hospice and palliative care for these Americans staggers the imagination.[4]

In 2007, it was estimated that every 72 seconds an American developed Alzheimer's disease;[5] and by mid-century, this diagnosis will be made every 33 seconds.[6] Unless medical science finds a way to prevent or to treat effectively this disease, the predictions are that by 2050, the number of individuals aged 65 and over with Alzheimer's could range from 11 million to 16 million.[7] The Medicine Payment Advisory Committee—an independent commission that advises Congress—reported that from 1998 to 2008, Alzheimer's and chronic dementia hospice cases grew from 28,000 to 174,000.[8]

In the United States, today, for Medicare Hospice Benefits to be activated, one must have a "terminal illness"[9] which means that a patient's medical prognosis is that he has only six months or less of life remaining.[10] Within some 39 pages in the Code of Federal Regulations,[11] procedures are laid out carefully for the administration of hospice care and the scope of financial responsibility for the government—for which Medicare covers nearly all costs associated with this care.[12] Throughout these policies and regulations, the stated goal for hospice care is to provide assistance which "optimizes quality of life by anticipating, preventing and treating suffering," and thereby "facilitate patient autonomy, access to information and choice" is unwavering.[13]

According to Medicare records, Medicare spending on hospice care from 2005 through 2009 rose 70% to $4.31 billion.[14] The Inspector General for the U.S. Department of Health and Human Services found for-profit hospices were paid 29% more per beneficiary than non-profit hospices. Medicare pays for 84% of all hospice patients.[15] All too frequently, for-profit hospices have been thought to "cherry pick" those patients who will live the longest and require the least amount of care—as for example, patients with dementia or Alzheimer's rather than those with cancer.[16]

Very often, palliative care practice seeks to manage incurable illness in "the least unpleasant course" and thereby allow a patient to die from their incurable illness in a manner which is the least traumatic.[17] In order for a

DOI: 10.1057/9781137377395

competent patient to exercise his autonomy and be informed sufficiently to determine the course of his medical treatment or non-treatment, an admittedly "gruesome discussion about ways of dying" must follow;[18] for, this then allows the patient to decide—essentially—which, of several terminal events, will end his life.[19] Understandably, some patients will not be willing, or psychologically capable, of entering into such a discussion.[20] In situations of this nature, the health care decision-makers must attempt to discern the patient wishes by evaluating the patient's "total good or best interests."[21] The challenge here is that if the patient is not informed, he cannot have a basis for formulating and evaluating ideas which promote his own best interests as he approaches his death.[22]

Political obstructions

When the United States Congress tackled this issue of advance planning consultations in debating the Patient Protection and Affordable Act,[23] high drama and near-hysterical rantings occurred over an irrational fear that discussions with one's general practitioners of this nature were little more than a precursor to end-stage decisions by so-called "death panels" regarding who would receive treatment and who would not.[24]

The Act was signed into law in March 2011, and did not include any provisions concerning end-of-life planning.[25] Rather, it was added initially to a complex Medicare-proposed regulation by the U.S. Department of Health and Human Services, setting payment rates for physicians' services during "annual wellness visits" for Medicare beneficiaries to include "advance care planning" for end-of-life management.[26] The final rule promulgated, however, excluded this very provision for consultation.[27]

End-of-life conversations: a national effort

The American Academy of Nursing has taken a leadership role in promoting a national dialogue aimed at educating the public as well as health professionals of the need for end-of-life conversations, which allow patient values and preferences for end-care and treatment to be discussed and considered before they become issues.[28] Ideally, this type of advance planning should occur rightfully among the supervisory care professionals, the involved patients, and their families.[29]

DOI: 10.1057/9781137377395

When forced to determine whether to offer life-prolonging and life-sustaining treatments to terminally ill autonomous patients, health care decision-makers should be guided by an evaluation of whether treatment measures are physiologically futile and the intrinsic burdens and risks they raise are overwhelmingly greater than their benefits;[30] or, in other words, is the treatment worse than the end-stage disease itself.

Concurrent treatment with palliative care

Normally, actual hospice care precludes curative treatment in end-of-life or terminal illness.[31] More contemporary thinking and policy, while acknowledging the primary goal of hospice care to provide comfort, symptom management and alleviation of pain, should not preclude actual treatment.[32] Traditionally, inter-disciplinary palliative care-teams of nurses, social workers, residents, and geriatricians, devote a major part of their work to maintaining a standard of qualitative living for patients with terminal illness. Oftentimes, a continuum of adjusted care is created from the initial diagnosis through the end-stage of illness.[33]

A distinct change in the actual scope of hospice care has been seen over the last ten years, which is beginning to embrace patients who are terminally ill and suffering with diseases other than cancer (e.g., dementia, chronic lung disease and congestive heart failure) and—as well—to provide palliative supplements for those patients who are terminally ill and confined to nursing homes.[34] In fact, presently, approximately one-third of hospitals in the United States are offering some form of in-patient palliative care which is not limited to life expectancy of six months or less.[35]

Nevertheless, because of prevailing requirements to forego disease-directed therapy before being allowed hospice care, most Americans die without the benefit of it.[36] "Bridge programs" are being experimented with, however, in some hospices which actually allow patients to continue active treatment therapies that are deemed important to the patient and of some limited potential for helping manage end-stage illness.[37]

Interestingly, there is an almost "hidden" provision within the Patient Protection and Affordable Care Act which allows for concurrent care.[38] Consequently, Medicare patients are allowed to continue conventional therapy while accessing hospice services.[39] The general thinking is that—given the time to make the transition from futile conventional therapies—most people will accept palliative care and hospice, thereby

DOI: 10.1057/9781137377395

benefitting themselves and, economically, in a *macro* sense, society at large.[40] In the final analysis, the better reasoned view is to consider palliative care and hospice care as "an integral part of all health care" and not as "care of last resort."[41]

The degree of care and level of sustainable qualitative living depends on disease prognosis. Some prognoses are poor, others terminal. While metastatic cancer is terminal, end-stage liver disease, severe emphysema and congestive heart failure are seen as conditions having limited rates of survival and often worse prognoses, as to time, than cancer. With a diagnosis of kidney disease, more often than not, this is seen as an appropriate time to develop strategies for end-stage care.[42]

It has been said that "the palliative care movement has come of age"—especially with the recent status of this care being certified as a sub-specialty by the American Board of Medical Specialties.[43] Even with these remarkable advances in expanded care and board certification of the field, there are not only gaps in providing adequate education and training in basic palliative management together but a shortage of skilled clinicians in this board-certified field.[44] Yet, it is hoped that this classification will serve as a catalyst for advancing greater opportunities for expanded training and service in palliative medicine.[45]

The contemporary reality of discerning a so-called "movement" toward palliative care was challenged significantly when the results of a study released in 2010 found that one-third of some 235,821 patients 65 years or older who were evaluated, spent their last days of life in hospitals and intensive-care units rather than being allowed to receive adequate palliative and hospice care.[46] Many of the patients admitted to hospice were so close to the days of their actual death that it was problematic whether the positive values of this type of care were even beneficial.[47]

The results of this study show, convincingly, that too many physicians are treating end-stage cancers far too aggressively and are, thus, failing to accept diagnosis and prognoses of medical futility and the merits of hospice care and palliative medicine in cases of this nature.[48] Even though surveys have shown 80% of cancer patients would prefer to die in their homes, this study found that the care "patients receive has less to do with what they want and more to do with the hospitals they happen to seek care."[49] Sadly, geography is, indeed, destiny.[50] As well, the receptivity of hospice care facilities to become directly involved with physician-assisted death choices by a patient will be determined by the specific hospice within which that patient enrolls.[51]

DOI: 10.1057/9781137377395

Fear, indecisiveness, or an abundance of caution

Interestingly, in Oregon, one of only three states having Death with Dignity legislation,[52] recent research on hospice care—an inference which may be extrapolated to a number of similar programs nationally—has revealed troubling conclusions.[53] No doubt one of the most disturbing facts from this research is that while 95.1% of the terminally ill patients in Oregon enrolled in hospice care in 2008–09,[54] only one in four resulting deaths occurred when life-ending medication was taken within the presence of an attending physician or a hospice staff member.[55] The assumption drawn, consequently, from this statistic is that a conflicting and compromising issue of patient care exists—particularly when set within the context of the popular understanding that hospice programs are "an important societal mechanism to assure that physician-assisted death is practiced responsibly."[56] Equally disturbing with this Oregon research was the fact that none of the hospices operating within the state assisted in all distinct phrases of the physician-assisted death process; indeed, a majority of Oregon hospices programs prohibit assistance.[57]

What is no doubt laid bare by this research is the center point of conflict for hospice care providers: namely adhering to the core values of hospice care (i.e., commitments to neither hasten nor postpone death) and—at the same time—being in full compliance with often vague and ambiguous legal standards, which have the effect of restraining efficacious medical care at the end-stage of life.[58] This paralysis of fear and indecision is unnecessary and misplaced when it comes to potential legal prosecutions for death assistance—this, simply because actions of this nature are seldom litigated.[59]

As between the concerns or tensions regarding the praxis of sound, common-sense medical care, respect for implementation of the principle of beneficence, and a moral sentiment and commitment of hospice care not to hasten death and/or euthanasia, these issues are magnified throughout the country and not found only in Oregon. An urgent need exists for hospice care providers to participate in a more open dialogue on the philosophy of adjusted care being realized in humane medical care for the dying. From this dialogue may come a new material policy of transparency which affords a more direct collaboration with patients seeking physician-assisted death within a hospice.[60]

DOI: 10.1057/9781137377395

The parameters of pain and existential suffering

Led by the World Health Organization, the International Association for the Study of Pain and its European Federation for Pain Study, a Global Day Against Pain was observed in October 2004, in Geneva, Switzerland.[61] This event marked an intensified effort to establish the relief of pain as a basic, fundamental human right and the recognition of chronic pain as a trans-national healthcare issue.[62]

Recognizing that the physical and psychosocial etiology of chronic pain sufferers manifests itself by, among other conditions, depression, anxiety, fear, and even suicide,[63] these three organizations defined pain recurring for a period of more than three months as chronic.[64] Not only do studies also disclose the significant employment irregularities resulting from chronic pain sufferers[65] but surveys of households in Europe and the United States revealed that 36% of Europeans may be classified as chronic pain sufferers; and in America, 43% of all households had members in chronic pain.[66] That percentage for Americans translated into a raw figure of 8 million. By 2030, it is expected this figure will double.[67]

Within this demographic is another projection which, if accurate, presages even greater stress on health care resources for the elderly and underscores the ultimate need for a system tuned to the needs of long-term end-of-life care. If, indeed, the over-65 population in the United States rises more than 70% between 2010 and 2030, and the payroll taxes for those within the general population rise, by then, to less than 4%, it is clear that planning efforts must be undertaken presently in order to meet these systematic needs.[68]

The WHO has developed a three-step "ladder" for cancer pain relief. In summary, it states:

> If pain occurs, there should be prompt oral administration of drugs in the following order: nonopioids (aspirin and paracetamol); then strong opioids such as morphine, until the patient is free of pain. To calm fears and anxiety, additional drugs—"adjuvants"—should be used. To maintain freedom from pain, drugs should be given 'by the clock,' that is every 3–6 hours, rather than 'on demand.' This three-step approach of administering the right drug in the right dose at the right time is inexpensive and 80–90% effective. Surgical intervention on appropriate nerves may provide further pain relief if drugs are not wholly effective.[69]

DOI: 10.1057/9781137377395

The President's Council on Bioethics concluded in 2005 that the basic standard for clinical decisionmaking should be one which promotes the best patient care.[70] This must, obviously, be adjusted continually as patient's case history progresses.[71] And, furthermore, it is care anchored in mercy, compassion, beneficence, or loving charity and care which recognizes that relief of pain is the most universal moral obligation that a physician must uphold and that there is, indeed, a right not to suffer.[72]

Psychological distress, or existential pain, is usually difficult to assess not only because it involves a substantial investment of physician time to determine or validate, but requires special training and contact with the families of patients.[73] There is a general societal aversion to proving a patient's emotional distress at end-of-life care.[74] Distinguishing between depression and psychologic morbidity is difficult as well because the sympathology of disrupted sleeping patterns, loss of energy and of appetite are response mechanisms to cancer and to other terminal illness and not just clear symptoms of deep psychological distress.[75] Because of these difficulties and uncertainties, the palliative management of existential pain has simply been neglected.[76]

While no general "solutions" exist for meeting the existential needs of terminally ill patients, attempts to meet these needs require careful listening skills and defined lines of communication among health care providers, patients, affected families and proxy or surrogate decision-makers. Valid existential concerns are, oftentimes, obscured and not brought into clear focus during palliative care treatment.[77] Even though a patient may have no absolute control over the wide and varied spectra of suffering, there is still freedom for a patient to choose what attitude is to be taken toward that suffering.[78] By extending end-of-life care to include psychiatric, psychological, existential and spiritual issues—consistent with the WHO's definition of palliative care and its goal of addressing total patient needs[79]—a more complete, compassionate, and realistic approach to managing terminal illness and end-stage suffering would be implemented.[80]

Assessing existential suffering

Interest in hastened death arises because a number of conditions exist: inadequate pain management, psychological conditions ranging from depression and hopelessness to fears of loss of control, autonomy, and physical functioning,[81] to futile and unbearable suffering, as well as avoidance of humiliation.[82] All of these conditions conduce to one over-riding fear: loss of human dignity,[83] which brings with it a fear of being forced to become but a "passive bystander" to all of the normal functions of life.[84] By acting to manage the dying process, which—for some—is viewed as too protracted and filled with growing and multiple functional losses,[85] a level of control is thereby exerted over a process which is acknowledged to be "by and large, a messy business."[86] And, sadly, this complicated and vexatious process for implementing the "new epidemiology of dying"[87] almost assures that heroic procedures will be followed which do not promote or sustain quality so much as postpone death.[88]

In approximately 25% of all terminally ill patients, depression and other mood disorders occur.[89] Yet, interestingly, few receive pharmacological aid by anti-depressant prescriptions.[90] As seen, the main obstacle to a more liberal response to these patients' needs is the lack of clarity in determining where a distressed, terminal patient is suffering from clinical depression or, is, instead, exhibiting a "normal grief response" to the dying process.[91] The components of both of these syndromes is often vague, imprecise and quite difficult to evaluate.[92] Commonly, when patients are obsessed with feelings of worthlessness, they lose their ability and desire to interact socially, and—indeed—lose their sense of hope, they are properly assessed as suffering from clinical depression[93] and should be given whatever drug dosage of analgesics deemed necessary to alleviate that condition—this, because pharmacotherapy is ultimately the principal tool for symptom control.[94]

Another drawback to accurate and prompt evaluations of psychological distress or existential suffering is, as observed, often the inability of a physician or palliative care management team to understand patient views about suffering. As a spiritual phenomena, suffering is often accepted as a meaningful and authentic community response to Christ's own suffering.[95] In some faith communities, cultural efforts are expended in order to view suffering—physically and mentally—as a positive, re-enforcing value.[96] Yet, merely because there is an acceptance of suffering as being authentic does not mean that suffering is, thus, meaningful.[97] It remains for the physician to ascertain and then listen carefully to the spiritual parameters within each patient's character[98] in an attempt to treat those seriously ill as "whole persons."[99] In this way, the therapy is truly patient-centered.[100]

DOI: 10.1057/9781137377395

Refractory existential suffering—or that symptomatology which defies adequate control despite all efforts to provide relief—is difficult, during the end stages of life, to distinguish from physical distress.[101] Those additional refractory symptoms most commonly reported as requiring attention by use of palliative sedation are: various degrees of agitation, restlessness or distress, confusion, respiratory distress, pain and myoclonus (e.g., severe twitching, jerking or uncontrollable shakes).[102]

Palliative sedation therapy is, thus, defined as "the use of sedative medications to relieve intolerable and refractory distress by the reduction in patient consciousness."[103] When patient suffering—physical or existential—becomes refractory to standard palliative therapies, the human, compassionate and merciful response is to offer terminal sedation.[104] This approach to medical treatment should be seen as consistent with sound principles of adjusted care.

Demoralization

It has been suggested that in the clinical setting of hospice or palliative care—a unique diagnostic category, termed the "demoralization syndrome," is becoming more recognizable and should be refined and classified as a cognitive disorder.[105] Seen as a "useful category of existential distress in which meaninglessness predominates and from which profound hopelessness and desire to die may result,"[106] this syndrome, if not supported satisfactorily by pharmacological therapy, should render such a demoralized patient incompetent to make medical decisions.[107]

Yet, interestingly, there is no conclusive empirical evidence to support an all-too-popular conclusion that depression so impairs judgment as to prevent one from making a competent decision to disapprove the initiation or cessation of medical treatment.[108] Sadly, this "depression argument" would appear to be but a ruse to both obstruct and even prevent end-of-life decisionmaking on grounds of moral repugnancy to alternative or surrogate health care providers.[109]

If and when the demoralization syndrome is accepted as a cognitive disorder, it would then remain for physicians to respond with compassion and with humaneness in remediating this medical condition. Accordingly, if deemed proper, medically, under the overarching principle of medical futility, physicians should consider the reasonableness of alleviating this pathological mental state in the end-stage patient by

DOI: 10.1057/9781137377395

administering terminal sedation. Such a course of treatment would be consistent with the central obligation of all physicians to alleviate pain and suffering—here, mental suffering—and to assure the dignity and safeguard the best interests of the dying.[110]

Notes

1 Bruce Jennings, True Rynders et al., *Access to Hospice Care: Expanding Boundaries, Overcoming Barriers*, 33 HASTINGS CENTER RPT. S3 (Special Supplement) (2003).

2 *Id.*

3 *Id.*

4 *Id.*
Current statistics show 5 million Americans are afflicted with dementia and more than 13 million are projected to be diagnosed by 2050. Susan L. Mitchell et al., *The Clinical Course of Advanced Dementia* 361 NEW ENG. J. MED. 1529, 1536 (Oct. 15, 2009).
  See generally JONATHAN HERRING, MEDICAL LAW AND ETHICS 506–07 (2nd ed., 2008) (calling for an expansion of palliative care options); Susan L. Mitchell, et al., *Hospice Care for Patients with Dementia.* 34 J. PAIN SYMPTOM MGT. 7 (2007).

5 Alzheimer's Association, *Alzheimer's Disease Facts and Figures* at 5 (2007).

6 *Id.*

7 *Id.*
Indeed, the World Health Organization projects, globally, dementia cases will triple to 115.4 million by 2050. Currently, estimated annual costs of care are set at $604 billion. Frank Jordans, *WHO: Dementia Cases Worldwide Will Triple by 2050*, WASH. EXAMINER, April 12, 2012, at 35.
  See Greg A. Sachs, *Dying from Dementia*, 361 NEW ENG. J. MED. 1595 (2009).

8 Kelly Kennedy, *Medicare Costs for Hospice up 70%*, USA TODAY, Aug. 8, 2011, at 1.
  See generally Nancy J. Knauer, *Aging in the United States: Re-thinking Justice, Equality, and Identity Across the Lifespan*, 21 TEMP. POL. & CIV. RTS. L. REV. 305 (2012).

9 42 C.F.R. §418.3 (2010).

10 42 C.F.R. §418.22(b) (2010).
  See Ezekiel J. Emanuel, *Better, if not Cheaper, Care*, N.Y. TIMES, Jan. 4. 2013, at A21 (suggesting a revision of the rules for admission to hospice—with an emphasis on a patient's need for specialized care rather than length of anticipated life).

DOI: 10.1057/9781137377395

See also Sachs, *supra* note 7, positing that end-stage dementia be treated only by palliative care; Pasman et al., *infra* Ch. 4 note 78, regarding limitations on providing nutrition and hydration to nursing home patients with this condition.

11   42 C.F.R. §§418.1–418.405 (2010).

12   *See* http://www.medicare.gov/publications/Pubs/pdf/02154.pdf (accessed Sept. 1, 2011). Current updates may be found at www.medicare.govt. Medicare provides coverage for two 90 day periods of hospice care— followed by an unlimited number of 60 day periods. The cap for this care is $6,500, adjusted for inflation or deflation. 42 C.F.R. §418.309 (2010).

In 2012, the Medicare program paid a base rate of $151 per day to cover all routine hospice services—adjusted, as such, for geographic differences. Melissa D. Aldridge Carlson et al., *Hospices' Enrollment Policies May Contribute to Underuse of Hospice Care in the United States*, 31 J. HEALTH AFFAIRS 2690 (2013).

13   42 C.F.R. §418.3 (2010).

14   Kennedy, *supra* note 8.

15   *Id.*

16   *Id.*

In a recent survey of some 600 hospices in the U.S., 78% had enrollment policies which allowed restrictions on access to care—especially for those with high-cost medical needs (e.g., patients receiving palliative radiation or blood transfusions or being fed intravenously). Specialized care can cost as much as $10,000.00 a month—and thus, exceed the Medicare hospice allowance. Carlson et al., *supra* note 12; Andrews *infra* note 36.

17   Fiona Randall and Robin S. Downie, Palliative Care Ethics: A Good Companion, 117 (1996).
See Stein Kaasa and Jon H. Loge, *Quality of Life in Palliative Care: Principles and Practice*, 17 Palliative Med. 11 (2003).

18   Randall and Downie, *id.* at 118.
It has predicted that 1 million Britons will become victims of dementia by 2023. Presently, the cost of the health and social care for each patient afflicted with dementia is £13.000 per year. Daniel Martin, *Dementia Timetable*, The Daily Mail, Feb. 4, 2010, at 12.

19   *Id.* at 117.
In a national poll of 1,000 U.S. citizens released on March 8, 2011, by the National Journal and The Regence Foundation, two key conclusions emerged: enhancing the quality of life for those seriously ill was accepted (by 71%) even though such action would shorten life, with 23% holding to the notion that every medical intervention should be taken; and more than half of those polled (55%) believed the health care system has both the responsibility and technology, together with the expertise, to offer whatever

DOI: 10.1057/9781137377395

treatments—regardless of the costs—to extend lives. *Living Well at the End of Life: A National Conversation*, (http://nationaljournal.com /events/event/45/).

Recent studies confirm that patients with end-stage illness are less likely to choose aggressive care when they fully understand what they can expect realistically. Amy Berman *infra* note 30.

20 Randall and Downie, *supra* note 17 at 118.

21 *Id.*
See *generally* Theresa Brown, Critical Care: A New Nurse Faces Death, Life And Everything In Between (2010).

22 Randall and Downie, *supra* note 17 at 119.
See Carl E. Schneider, The Practice Of Autonomy: Patients, Doctors, And Medical Decisions 175 *passim* (1996).

23 Pub. L. No. 111–48, 124 Stat. 119 (2010) (to be codified as amended in scattered sections of 21, 25, 26, 29 and 42 U.S.C.).
A PDF of this Act may be found at http://www.gpo.gov/fdsys/pkg/PLAW-111publ48/pdf/PLAW-111publ48.pdf.

24 Evan Thomas, *infra*, note 36.
The poll taken by The Regence Foundation and the National Journal (*supra* note 19) found—contrary to the political stance taken by Congress on advance planning conversations—that three out of four Americans (or 78% of those polled) were not only interested in being more educated to end-of-life medical treatment options but thought this topic should be a priority for the U.S. health care system and covered by both Medicare and by private insurance. *See* http://www.getpalliativecare.org/; Matthew DoBias, *No Death Panels, Please, But Poll Shows Americans Can Handle End-of-Life Care*, Nat'l Journal, Mar. 8, 2011, http://nationaljournal.com/healthcare/no-death-panels-please-but-poll-shows-americans-c...
See *generally* Abigail R. Moncrief, *The Freedom of Health*, 159 Pa. L. Rev. 2210 at 2238–41 (2011).

25 Robert Pear, *U.S. Alters Rule on Paying End-of-Life Planning*, N.Y. Times, Jan. 4, 2011, at A15.

26 *Id.*

27 *Id.*

28 American Academy of Nursing, Policy Brief, *Advance Care Planning as a Urgent Public Concern*, April 26, 2010.
See Mitchell, *The Clinical Course of Advanced Dementia*, *supra* note 4 (concluding that patients with advanced dementia who were able to discuss the disease's prognosis with their health care proxies received less burdensome interventions than those whose proxies who did not understand the expected complications).

DOI: 10.1057/9781137377395

See also Allan E. Buchanan and Dan W. Brock, Deciding for Others: The Ethics of Surrogate Decision Making, 281 (1989); Joe Klein, *How to Die*, Time at 18 (June 11, 2012).

29   American Academy of Nursing, *id.*
     See Maria J. Silveira et al., *Advance Directives and Outcomes of Surrogate Decision Making before Death*, 362 New Eng. J. Med. 1211 (April 1, 2010); Annette Rid and David Wendler, *Can We Improve Treatment Decision-Making for Incapacitated Patients?*, 40 Hastings Center Rpt. 36 (2010).

30   Randall and Downie, *supra* note 17 at 119; Kaasa and Loge, *supra* note 17.
     See Amy Berman, *At the End, Peace*, Wash. Post, May 1, 2012, at E1.

31   Sandra L. Ragan, et al., *The Communication of Palliative Care for The Elderly Cancer Patient*, 15 Health Communication 219 (2003).

32   *Id.*
     See Kathleen Tschantz and Diane E. Meier, *Palliative Care and Hospice: Opportunities to Improve Care for the Sickest Patients*, 25 Notre Dame J. L. Ethics & Pub. Pol'y, 413 (2011).

33   Joanne Kenen, *A New Focus on Easing the Pain: Palliative Care Helps The Very Ill. It May Also Keep Costs Down*, Wash. Post, July 3, 2007, at F1.

34   Timothy E. Quill, *Physician-Assisted Death in the United States: Are the Existing 'Last Resorts' Enough?* 38 Hastings Center Rpt. 17 (Sept.–Oct. 2008).

35   Kenen *supra*, note 33.
     See Theresa Brown, *Looking for a Place to Die*, N.Y. Times, Dec. 22, 2011, at A33 (discussing issues associated with moving from a hospital ICU to in-patient hospice care or patient home care); Klein, *supra* note 28.

36   Quill, *supra* note 34.
     While approximately 70% of Americans wish to die at home, about half die in hospitals; and although hospice or palliative care is available to those suffering from terminal illness, practically, most get only a few weeks of this care. Evan Thomas, *The Case for Killing Granny: Re-Thinking End-of-Life Care*, Newsweek, Sept. 21, 2009, at 34, 40. Home hospice care is the standard. Michelle Andrews, *Hospice providers may have financial reasons to discourage the enrollment of certain patients*, WASH. POST, Jan. 22, 2013 at E4.

37   Quill, *supra* note 34.
     Interestingly, the Medicare Payment Advisory Committee's 2011 Report to Congress found 44% of patients transferred back to traditional care from hospices and thus exceeded the six month spending cap on Medicare hospice funding. This statistic suggests some hospices may be admitting patients before they actually meet the eligibility requirement. Ongoing consideration is being given to reducing payments for hospice in nursing facilities. An increasing number of hospices are collecting the same daily rate for visiting patients in nursing facilities as other hospice programs which provide, as

DOI: 10.1057/9781137377395

well, patients' room, board and medical care not related to their terminal illness. Kennedy, *supra* note 8.

38   124 Stat. § 3140.
The Act is codified at 42 U.S.C. §§ 18001 *et seq.* (2011).

39   *Id.*

40   Eleanor Clift, *Hospice and The End Game*, 30 HEALTH AFFAIRS 1606, 1609 (Aug. 2011).
One recent study of four New York State hospitals found well-established palliative care-teams for Medicaid patients reduced in-patient costs and time spent in intensive-care units by $6,900.00 per admission. R. Sean Morrison et al., *Palliative Care Consultant in Teams Cut Hospital Costs for Medicaid Beneficiaries*, 30 HEALTH AFFAIRS 454 (Mar. 2011).

41   Jennings et al., *supra* note 1 at S9.
A recent report by the Lien Foundation on end-of-life care in 40 countries found Britain topped the list with Australia placing second and the United States third. Three factors were ranked: life expectancy, hospice availability, and access to painkillers. Because of the policy by health insurers that payment for palliative care will only be covered when a patient relinquishes curative treatments upon entering hospice, the United States did not score well on this assessment factor. *See Grim Reapings: The Quality of Death*, THE ECONOMIST, July 17, 2010, at 54.

42   Kenen, *supra* note 33.
See PALLIATIVE CARE: TRANSFORMING THE CARE OF SERIOUS ILLNESS (Diane E. Meier et al., eds. 2010); David Hui et al., *Availability and Integration of Palliative Care at U.S. Cancer Centers*, 303 JAMA 1054 (Mar. 17, 2010).

43   Quill, *supra* note 34 at 16.

44   *Id.* at 18.

45   *Id.*
See Emanuel, *supra* note 10 (urging all hospitals to have palliative care units and not just 40% of present ones which have more than 50 beds).
A comprehensive website on palliative medicine authored by the American Academy of Hospice and Palliative Medicine may be found at: http://www.aahpm.org/news /default/news6.html.

46   Rob Stein, *Wide Disparities are found in End-Stage Cancer Treatment*, WASH. POST, Nov. 17, 2010, at A7.

47   *Id.*

48   *Id.*
But see Elizabeth Trice Loggers, Helene Stacks et al., *Implementing a Death with Dignity Program at a Comprehensive Cancer Center*, 368 NEW ENG. J. MED. 1417 (April 11, 2013) (comparing the successful programs of this nature in Oregon and Washington).

DOI: 10.1057/9781137377395

49 Quill, *supra* note 34 at 16.

    See generally Berman, *supra* note 30; The Pew Research Center Survey, Nov. 2005, *The Right to Die*, (Press Release, Jan. 5, 2006).

50 *Id. But see* Kellen F. Rodriguez, *Suing Health Care Providers for Saving Lives: Liability for Providing Unwanted Life-Sustaining Treatment*, 20 J. LEGAL MED. 1 (1999).

51 Courtney S. Campbell and Jessica Cox, *Hospice and Physician-Assisted Death: Collaboration, Compliance, and Complicity*, 40 HASTINGS CENTER RPT. 26, 34 (Sept.–Oct. 2010).

52 ORE. REV. STAT., §§ 127.800(12), 127.805 (2009).

    The other state with comparable legislation is Washington. *See* REV. CODE WASH. ANN., Ch. 70, 245 (2009).

    Vermont passed similar legislation May 13, 2013. 18 VT. STAT. ANN. Ch. 113, §5281.

    A ballot initiative in Massachusetts which would have followed the legislation in Oregon and Washington on death assistance was defeated. Carolyn Johnson, *Assisted Suicide Measure Narrowly Defeated; Supporters Concede Defeat*, THE BOSTON GLOBE, Nov. 7, 2012, at http://www.boston.com/2012/11/07/dying/gBqan95E7zK3elChciPBOP/story.html. *See* Ch. 5, *infra*, notes 5–7.

53 Campbell and Cox, *supra* note 51.

54 *Id.* at 26.

55 *Id.* at 34.

56 *Id.* at 27.

57 *Id.* at 31, 34.

58 *Id.*

59 *See* Alan Meisel, *infra*, Ch. 5, note 21.

60 Campbell and Cox, *supra* note 51 at 34.

61 Arthur G. Lipman, *Pain as a Human Right: The 2004 Global Day Against Pain*, 19 J. PAIN & PALLIATIVE CARE PHARMACOTHERAPY 85 (2005).

62 *Id.*

    See Laura Thomas et al., *Access to Pain Treatment and Palliative Care: A Human Rights Analysis*, 24 TEMP. INT'L. & COMP. L. J. 365 (2010).

    In the U.S., the American Pain Foundation is the largest non-profit advocacy group for pain patients working as such to preserve access to drugs without making patients being made to feel as though they are criminals and to combat notions that opiod addition is rampant especially among the terminally ill. Charles Ornstein and Tracy Weber, *Success of Pain Killer Funds Patient Advocacy Group, Probe Finds*, WASH. POST, Dec. 25, 2011, at A4.

    The web page for the Pain Foundation is: http://www.painfoundation.com.

63 Lipman, *id.* at 86.

64 *Id.* at 88.

DOI: 10.1057/9781137377395

65 *Id.* at 89.

66 *Id.* at 88.

67 *Access to Hospice Care: Expanding Boundaries, Overcoming Boundaries*, 33 HASTINGS CENTER RPT. S 50 (Mar.–April, 2003).
Statistics showed in 2010 that $8.5 billion worth of narcotic pain killers were sold in the U.S.—this, being enough prescription drugs to "medicate every American around the clock" for a month—and, thus, fuel concerns that there is a drug "epidemic." Ornstein and Weber, *supra* note 62.

See Catherine Saint Louis, *E.R. Doctors Face Dilemma on Painkillers*, NEW YORK TIMES, May 21, 2012, at D1; Barry Meier, *Tightening the Lid on Pain Prescription*, WASH. POST, April 9, 2012, at 12 (detailing how there are more and more state laws—and especially in Washington—being enacted to control the grossly over prescribed practice of treating with opiods for long-term pain, from back injuries and other non cancerous conditions, by first requiring patients taking these drugs to consult pain specialists to learn whether there are alternative approaches to pain abatement); Ch. 5, *infra*, note 71.

See also Timothy W. Martin, *Nurses Seek Expanded Role: Specialists in Anesthesia Want to Treat Chronic Pain; Critics Warn of Drug Abuse*, WALL ST. J. Oct. 3, 2012, at A3 (reporting on the Centers for Medicare and Medical Services issuance of a new guideline allowing nurse anesthetists to be directly reimbursed by Medicare for evaluating, diagnosing, and treating pain with epidural injects of prescription painkillers or opioids thereby responding to the public demand for greater access to medication for chronic pain). This new rule, 42 C.F.R 410.69(b), became effective January 1, 2013. Reimbursements allowed under it are conditioned, however, by individual state scope of practice laws (77 Fed. Reg. 69006). Some 24 states allow nurse anesthetists to provide some level of chronic pain treatment. *Id.*

68 *Access to Hospice Care, id.*
It is estimated that in order to support Medicare and Medicaid program costs, payroll taxes must meet four percent. *Id.*

69 WHO, Pain Relief Ladder, http://www.who.int/cancer/palliative/painladder/en/index.html.

70 President's Council on Bioethics, TAKING CARE: ETHICAL CARE GIVING IN OUR AGING SOCIETY 217 (2005).
Best patient care is adjusted to the developing medical needs of the patient. Essential to the standard of best care is acceptance of the "intrinsic dignity of persons" which, in turn, mandates that the goal of providing care must be to enhance total patient well being (somatic and non somatic) and, at the end-of-life demonstrate beneficence, compassion, or charity in managing pain and suffering. DAVID C. THOMASMA, HUMAN LIFE IN THE BALANCE, 165, 184 (1990).

DOI: 10.1057/9781137377395

See EDMUND D. PELLEGRINO and DAVID C. THOMASMA, FOR THE PATIENT'S GOOD: THE RESTORATION OF BENEFICENCE IN HEALTH CARE Chs. 2, 5 (1988).

See also DAVID C. THOMASMA and GLENN C. GRABER EUTHANASIA: TOWARD AN ETHICAL SOCIAL POLICY 192 *passim* (1991) for a discussion of the principle of adjusted care.

71   THOMASMA and GRABER, *id.* at 129.

72   *Id.* at 192, 194 (quoting Dr. Edmund D. Pellegrino).

73   Manish Agrawal and Ezekiel J. Emmanuel, *Attending to Psychologic Symptoms and Palliative Care*, 20 J. CLINICAL ONCOLOGY 624 (Feb. 1, 2001).

74   *Id.*
     See generally Paul Arnstein, et al., *Self Efficacy as a Mediator of The Relationship between Pain Intensity, Disability and Depression in Chronic Pain Patients*, 80 PAIN 483 (1999).

75   Put simply, the dying "do not have the luxury of clearly separating their physical suffering from their psychological, spiritual, an existential suffering." Timothy E. Quill and Margaret P. Battin, *Excellent Palliative Care as The Standard, Physician Assisted Dying as a Last Resort*, at 323 in PHYSICIAN-ASSISTED DYING, (Timothy E. Quill and Margaret P. Battin eds. 2004).

76   Agrawal and Emmanuel, *supra* note 73.

77   Ingrid Bolmsjo, et al., *Meeting Existential Needs in Palliative Care—Who, When, and Why?*, 18 J. PALLIATIVE CARE 185 (2002).

78   William Breitbart, et al., *Psychotherapeutic Interventions at The End of Life: A Focus on Meaning and Spirituality*, 49 CAN. J. PSYCHIATRY 336 (June, 2004).

79   Cicely Saunders, *Hospice*, 1 MORTALITY 317, 320 (1996).

80   Breitbart et al., *supra* note 78 at 371.
     See Arthur Kleinman, *From Illness as Culture to Caregiving as Moral Experience*, 368 NEW ENG. J. MED. 1376 (April 2013).

81   Helene Stacks et al., *Why Now? Timing and Circumstances of Hastened Deaths*, 30 J. PAIN & SYMPTOM MGT. 216 (Sept. 2005).

82   G. Van der Wal and R. J. M. Dillman, *Euthanasia in The Netherlands*, 308 BR. MED. J. 1346 (1994).

83   DEREK HUMPHRY, FINAL EXITS 135–36 (1991).

84   Richard B. Gunderman, *Is Suffering the Enemy?*, 32 HASTINGS CENTER RPT. 40, 42 (Mar.–April 2002).

85   Stacks et al., *supra* note 81.

86   SHERWIN B. NULAND, HOW WE DIE: REFLECTIONS ON LIFE'S FINAL CHAPTER at 142 (1994).

87   *Id.* at 12.

88   JOANNE LYNN, SICK TO DEATH AND NOT GOING TO TAKE IT ANYMORE 164–65 (2004).

89   Karel E. Miller, et al., *Anti depressant Medication Use in Palliative Care*, 23 AM. J. HOSPICE & PALLIATIVE MED. 127 (Mar.–April 2006).

DOI: 10.1057/9781137377395

90   *Id.*
     Some other earlier studies have, however, shown that a number of
     terminally ill cancer patients have—indeed—received sedation for
     psychological or mental agonies. Tatsuya Morita, et al., *Terminal Sedation
     for Existential Distres*s, 17 AM. J. HOSPICE & PALLIATIVE CARE 189, n's
     4, 6–8. A 1996 study done of experts on sedation in the U.K. and America
     found that in 22% of cases evaluated, sedation was administered because
     of patient "anguish" and in 16% of cases, it was undertaken because of the
     "emotional, psychological [or] spiritual distress" of those patients. Susan
     Chater,
     et al., *Sedation for Intractable Distress in the Dying—a Survey of Experts*, 12
     PALLIATIVE MED. 255 (1998).
91   Miller, et al., *supra* note 89.
92   *Id.*
93   *Id.* at 128.
94   Arthur G. Lipman, *The Scream by Edvard Munch: A Profound Portrayal of
     Existential Pain*, 19 J. PAIN & PALLIATIVE CARE PHARMACOTHERAPY
     1, 2 (2005).
95   Stan Van Hooft, *The Meanings of Suffering*, 28 HASTINGS CENTER RPT. 13
     (1998).
     See generally STANLEY HAUERWAS, GOD, MEDICINE AND
     SUFFERING, Chs. II, III (1990).
96   Van Hooft, *id.* at 14.
97   *Id.* at 15.
98   Seth M. Holmes, et al., *Screening the Soul: Communication Regarding Spiritual
     Concerns Among Primary Care Physicians and Seriously Ill Patients Approaching
     the End of Life*, 23 AM. J. HOSPICE & PALLIATIVE MED. 25, 30 (2006).
99   Alton Hart, Jr., et al., *Hospice Patient's Attitudes Regarding Spiritual Discussion
     with Their Donors*, 20 AM. J. HOSP. PALLIATIVE CARE 135 (2003).
100 Holmes et al., *supra* note 98.
     See generally Alan B. Astrow and Daniel P. Sulmasy, *Spirituality and The
     Patient-Physician Relationship*, 291 JAMA 2884 (2004).
101 Paul Rousseau, *Existential Suffering and Palliative Sedation: A Brief
     Commentary with a Proposal for Clinical Guidelines*, 18 AM. J. HOSPICE &
     PALLIATIVE CARE 151 (May/June 2001).
     See James Halenbeck, *Terminal Sedation for Intractable Distress: Not Slow
     Euthanasia but a Prompt Response to Suffering*, 171 WESTERN J. MED. 222
     (Oct. 1999).
102 Bernard Lo and Gordon Rubenfeld, *Palliative Sedation in Dying Patients: 'We
     Turn to it When Everything Else Hasn't Worked'*, 294 JAMA 1810, 1811 (Oct. 12,
     2005).
     See generally Joseph W. Shega, et al., *Patients Dying with Dementia: Experience*

DOI: 10.1057/9781137377395

at the End of Life and Impact on Hospice Care, 35 J. PAIN SYMPTOM MGT. 499 (2008) (conducting a study that showed patients with dementia who enroll in hospice programs may experience better end-of-life care, though certain "nontreatable" symptoms still persist and cause the majority of distress for patients).

103   Tatsuya Morita, et al., *Definition of Sedation for Symptom Relief: A Systematic Literature Review and a Proposal for Operational Criteria*, 24 J. PAIN & SYMPTOM MGT. 447 (Oct. 4, 2002).

104   Rousseau, *supra* note 101; P.C. Rousseau, *Dying and Terminal Sedation*, 7 CLIN. GERIATRICS 19 (1999).

105   David W. Kissane, *The Contribution of Demoralization to End of Life Decisionmaking*, 34 HASTINGS CENTER RPT. 21, 24 (July–Aug., 2004).

106   *Id.* at 23.
While anxiety and depression are viewed as "expressions of mortality"—thereby making them "synonymous with suffering (and) existential distress," demoralization may occur "independently of depression." *Id.* at 23, 24.

107   *Id.* at 29.

108   RONALD A. LINDSAY, FUTURE BIOETHICS: OVERCOMING TABOOS, MYTHS AND DOGMAS 111 (2008).

109   *Id.* at 112.

110   THOMASMA and GRABER, *supra* note 70 at 192, 194 (quoting Dr. Edmund D. Pellegrino).
All too often those in the end-stage of life and suffering with dementia, receive an array of aggressive therapies from forced tube feeding to hospitalization for pneumonia—all of which are not only of limited benefit but inconsistent with sound standards of palliative management. Mitchell, et al., *supra* note 4 at 1535.

DOI: 10.1057/9781137377395

2

Total Pain Management and Adjusted Care: An Evolving Ideal

Abstract: *This chapter develops the theme of managing somatic pain and existential suffering by examining the principle of total pain management which has been seen as integral to palliative care and, thus, requires palliating the whole person by managing physical, psychosocial, and spiritual dimensions of suffering. What is needed is a more uniform adoption of standards and protocols which allow regular use of palliative or "terminal" sedation as a valid component of adjusted care—without professional censure or threat of legal sanction for "euthanizing" or assisting in suicide. When use of terminal sedation is consistent with individual patient values and in the best medical interests of the patients to relieve end-stage pain and suffering, it should be seen as but a proportionate response to patient suffering.*

George P. Smith. *Palliative Care and End-of-Life Decisions.* New York: Palgrave Macmillan, 2013. DOI: 10.1057/9781137377395.

Long before Soren Kierkegaard first tackled the issue of existential pain,[1] or what today is often termed psychological distress or suffering,[2] the concept and reality of such a dimension or level of pain at death was perhaps first recorded in the Bible when Jesus, in contemplating his own death, stated, "I am deeply grieved, even to death....."[3] No doubt, Edvard Munch's artistic depiction of "The Scream" may well be taken as the most profound artistic depiction of existential suffering ever rendered in oil.[4] Indeed, it has been recognized as capturing an "intense state of anxiety and despair" where "loss of identity becomes death."[5] While art confers an unmistakable visibility on distress in its varied complex forms, literature rarely captures it adequately—this, because pain "resists verbal objectification" as there is no language for it.[6]

Without question, pain plays havoc with the human psyche and induces suffering which, having no meaning, can destroy.[7] Indeed, denying "suffering is to trivialize another person's experience, to diminish its scope and lessen its significance."[8] Once it can be shown that there is a right to compassionate care—as this book advocates—accepting and validating this new right would, perforce, trigger a co-ordinating duty to make judgments relative to quality of life in order to assess the extent of one's suffering. In a very real way, then, a right of compassionate care would embrace and incorporate this collateral duty to prevent suffering.[9] Central to the enforcement of a right to compassionate care for terminal illness at the end-stage of life, then, is acceptance of an ethic of care which requires a "provision for competent care,"[10] which is adjusted to on-going medical needs as a patient's illness progresses and which, thereby, meets the fundamental goal of medicine which is to relieve suffering.[11]

Although existential pain has been defined as suffering "with no clear connections to physical pain," it has also been recognized as suffering which can in fact be expressed as physical pain.[12] It is seen further as a significant clinical factor which may either reinforce existing physical pain or be the root cause of physical pain.[13]

From the very beginnings of the hospice movement in the United Kingdom led by Dame Cicely Saunders in 1967,[14] "total pain" management of physical, psychosocial and spiritual suffering was then—and is today—the goal of hospice care.[15] Palliating the whole person and offering compassionate care[16] is central to hospice care.[17] Viewed as such, palliative care presents an alternative not only to assisted suicide and active, voluntary euthanasia, but to the compulsiveness of some health care providers who forever press active "curative" care and treatments when

DOI: 10.1057/9781137377395

they are medically inappropriate or *contra* indicated.[18] In this regard, hospice care is an effort to counterbalance this irrational and inhumane compulsiveness and thereby "humanize medicine."[19]

Palliative care is care which does not effect a cure and is defined by the World Health Organization as that care which "improves the quality of life for patients and families who face life-threatening illness, by providing pain and symptom relief, spiritual and psychosocial support from diagnosis to the end of life and bereavement."[20] Palliating the whole person, then, requires medicine to attend more fully to the phenomenon of existential pain. For this to be efficacious, regular re-assessments of patient treatment goals must be undertaken. From these communications, the health care decision-makers will not only learn directly from their patient how they define and experience suffering but their thresholds for tolerating various sources of distress. These thresholds are seen as being informed by a patient's personality which has, in turn, been shaped by life experiences and attitudes toward death management and quality of life in end-stage illness.[21]

Medical futility and terminal sedation

It has been argued that death should never be sought or engineered as a "therapeutic option" to end suffering.[22] Yet, when the prolongation of life-sustaining treatments impose undue burdens or serve as futile roadblocks to one in the medically validated end-stage of life,[23] thereby preventing as "comfortable" a death as possible,[24] palliative care—it is asserted in this book—should include an unencumbered option of respite or, what is also termed, terminal sedation as a compassionate response to such situations. Accordingly, fulfilling the ethical mandate to prevent pain and suffering, health care providers should standardize a protocol which allows them—with patient or family approval—or, when a patient is unconscious and without proxy decision maker—to take those reasonable steps to relieve unremitting pain and discomfort.[25] The thesis of this book is that law and medicine must agree on set standards or adopt protocols which allow for—without professional censure or legal retribution—the use of terminal sedation as an efficacious and compassionate practice for end-stage treatment of patients.

Existing medico-legal and ethical norms allow, in limited circumstances, the terminal sedation of a dying patient.[26] Indeed, it is

DOI: 10.1057/9781137377395

acceptable and compassionate to sedate a patient in terminal distress when this action is undertaken to "produce unconsciousness before extubation;" to relieve physical suffering when standard palliative care does not abate refractory symptoms "and possibly" when non-physical suffering is sought to be relieved.[27] Yet, in order for a physician to engage in terminal sedation, he must not intend by doing so to end the life of his patient.[28] Rather, if a patient dies from high dosages of sedating medications, the medications must be given with the intent to relieve pain rather than cause death—although death is a foreseeable risk.[29] This is known as the doctrine of double effect, a well-established and nearly universally accepted principle of medical ethics and related law.[30]

Troublesome as the doctrine of double effect is as a construct for discerning physician intent, notably, the American Medical Association—through its Council on Ethics and Judicial Affairs—still clings to the doctrine as determinative in justifying the use of terminal sedation.[31] What is submitted is that rather than being mired, compulsively, in efforts to discern and validate positive subjective intentions for use of terminal sedation by a physician, a decision is made which—based on sound and accepted medical judgment—weighs directly the costs versus the benefits of treatments in this manner.[32]

Common sense and compassion

Wider acceptance and use of terminal sedation as a valid method of palliative treatment presents an important opportunity for a fuller understanding of the issues of managing death and an equal opportunity for viewing this medical procedure as a compromise to the equally vexatious issue of physician-assisted suicide.[33] Taxonomical confusion abounds when issues of self-determination are presented in end-stage illness.[34] Clarity in praxis could truly carry transformative power to abate confusion here as well as to educate—particularly since there is often a tragic absence of explicit policies which enunciate clearly the extent to which care may be provided to the terminally ill.[35]

The voluntary cessation of nutrition and hydration and the use of terminal sedation are acknowledged as legal and accepted widely in hospice care management.[36] Because of an absence of clear protocols on its administration as well as moral objections to its use and legal concerns of the consequences of ordering its use, terminal sedation is not readily available.[37] Although illegal in all states but Oregon,[38] and Washington,[39] physician-assisted suicide is difficult to prosecute successfully when requested by a competent and informed patient.[40] Voluntary euthanasia is also illegal and, if uncovered, likely to be prosecuted.[41] Because of this legal situation, a vast underground flourishes which assists not only in the practice of physician-assisted suicide but voluntary euthanasia.[42]

Although physician-assisted death is not to be considered a substantive liberty interest and a fundamental right,[43] nor is palliative care seen as a "right" incorporated into a lofty constitutional principle,[44] it is argued here that both actions coalesce into actuating a right to be free from intolerable and unmanageable pain and suffering—a right which the U.S. Supreme Court has said exists[45] and is grounded in the essential right to refuse life-sustaining treatment.[46]

Rather than continue to be overwhelmed with vexatious and often contrived issues, what should be uppermost is—in cases of intractable end-stage terminal suffering—a rational approach to legal decisionmaking.[47] This approach should be guided by what, clinically, is judged to be in the best interests of the patient in order to maintain his dignity, comfort, and promote a standard of beneficence during his final days.[48]

Perfect solutions for clinical dilemmas do not exist, nor can medicine sanitize death. When pain is refractory and unremitting suffering follows despite efforts to palliate a patient's medical condition, although "imperfect," terminal sedation and the voluntary refusal of nutrition and hydration are valid courses of action to follow and have the ultimate effect of enhancing patient autonomy.[49]

Interestingly, up to 90% of pain can be controlled by analgesics.[50] Yet, for hospice care patients who suffer severe pain during the last week of life which is set in a range from 5%–35% (with 25% experiencing unbearable shortness of breath), the 90% statistical success is unimpressive.[51] Indeed, previous scholarship reported significant pain, among end-stage patients, to be as high as 50%.[52]

Rather than investigating the linguistic, moral, and philosophical ambiguities as well as the awkward consequences inherent with the voluntary cessation of nutrition and hydration, terminal sedation, physician-assisted suicides and voluntary active euthanasia,[53] this book advances the hypothesis that there is an inextricable component or commonality to evaluating and implementing each of these four actions designed to hasten a humane death: namely, common sense and

DOI: 10.1057/9781137377395

compassion. In turn, this policy is rooted in the biomedical principle of beneficence[54] which is tied to the notion that there is a human right to compassionate care in end-of-life illness[55]—with suffering being seen, properly, to include physical *and* psychological distress.[56] The proper or controlling inquiry to be made with any of these four actions is, quite simply, whether these procedures are consistent with sound medical practice and thus are in the best medical interests of the patients to relieve end-stage physical and/or mental suffering. Stated otherwise, the overarching strategic issue and—indeed—the conclusion to be reached is the extent to which any of these courses of action is a proportional response to patient suffering, they should be viewed, legally and medically, as proper acts of compassion and efficacious forms of relieving intractable end-stage pain and suffering.

Codifying clinical epidemiologies

With enlightened clinical policies or protocols setting forth standards for the use of terminal or respite sedation as a proportional response to the complex spectrum of pain and suffering associated with end-stage illness, palliative care will then have a broadened focus or sphere of application and not be shackled rigidly to being shaped or controlled unnecessarily by the principle of double effect. Rather than question the integrity of terminal sedation, its wider acceptance is compatible with the principle of adjusted care[57] for all medical treatment and, as well, both a reasoned and compassionate response to managing medically futile cases.[58]

Once terminal sedation is accepted and used more widely as a valid medical procedure within the sound tenets of palliative care and made, accordingly, more readily available to alleviate psychological distress in end-stage illness, the next step is broadening the clinical outreach of terminal sedation to evaluate the validity for use in cases of non-terminal psychiatric illness.[59] It is not within the scope of analysis of this book to investigate this issue in depth. It is, however, important to make several observations which might well shape the course of policy debate as it must eventually be shaped in order to resolve this issue. Indeed, the proper laws for structuring normative standards must continue to be explored, then debated, and subsequently refined over the succeeding years.

DOI: 10.1057/9781137377395

European approaches to psychogenic pain

Interestingly, Belgium, the Netherlands,[60] and—more recently—Switzerland[61] have allowed compassionate medical assistance in those cases where non-terminal patients have endured a constant (or permanent) level of mental suffering which qualifies as a chronic mental illness (e.g., manic/depressive or bipolar) after years of "debilitating anxiety" or even possibly "agonies of rheumatoid arthritis."[62] The Swiss Federal Supreme Court issued a ruling in 2006 under which for the first time, assisted suicide is to be available to psychiatric patients and others with mental illness who suffer from "incurable, permanent, severe psychological disturbances" as well as to those with severe, long-term mental illness who have made "rational" and "well considered" decisions to end their lives in order to avoid further suffering.[63] In 1995, the Royal Dutch Medical Association determined that no valid distinction is to be drawn between physical and mental suffering.[64] Yet, the Association cautioned that in making medical evaluations of non-somatic illness, great care and caution should be exercised in assessing both the gravity and the depth of hopelessness consequential to the primary medical condition.[65]

Legislative efforts in the British Parliament—led by Baron Joel Joffe—to enact an Assisted Dying for the Terminally Ill Act in 2006 came to naught.[66] This proposal sought to allow terminally ill patients medical assistance in ending their lives and, in this regard, was patterned after similar successful legislation of this activity in Oregon.[67]

In an effort to bring clarity and stability to the debate on death assistance, on February 25, 2010, the British Crown Prosecution Service issued a document entitled, *Policy for Prosecutors in Respect of Cases of Encouraging Assisting Suicide.* Attempting to resolve moral ambiguities in cases of assisted suicide and mercy killings, the guidelines nonetheless fail to address not only the condition or degree of suffering the person requesting the suicide is experiencing but also do not address the situation in which a patient is neither terminally ill nor disabled but is suffering from severe depression or psychological distress. The guidelines do not change the law prohibiting assisted suicide. Rather, they provide guidance on which cases are likely to be prosecuted. They attempt to distinguish between "compassionate support" for which there would be a less likelihood of prosecution from cases of "malicious encouragement" which would be prosecuted.[68]

DOI: 10.1057/9781137377395

Interestingly, the first case investigation under these guidelines, in 2010, involved a 79-year-old physician, Dr. Michael Irwin, who provided death management assistance to some 12 patients. Although sufficient evidence was presented which could have provided a conviction under the Suicide Act of 1961, it was determined that the public interest would not be served by prosecuting a senior physician who claimed that he acted with compassion—consistent with the standards set under the assistance with suicide guidelines.[69]

Previously, in another British case determined in 2004, it was held that a woman suffering from a terminal medical condition—cerebella ataxia—who wished to travel to Switzerland with the assistance of her husband to be euthanized, could not be enjoined from such a course of action.[70] Although the Suicide Act of 1961 would, indeed, criminalize the actions of the woman's husband because they would aid or abet her illegal act of suicide, the law of suicide did not criminalize the conduct. The court concluded that although Parliament may criminalize an act, "it is not always in the public interest to prosecute in respect of it."[71]

Relative Assisted Suicide (RAS), and—more specifically Relative Facilitating Suicide Abroad (RFASA), has the real potential if accepted legislatively and judicially of resolving—to a considerable extent—the furor over physician-assisted death. Indeed, when British prosecutors have essentially given a relative exemption for assisting terminally ill family members, in some limited number of cases, they have advanced the de-medicalization of assisted dying and thereby relegated the role of the physician to that of determining the competency of the terminal, end-of-life person to request assistance in dying and providing a drug prescription to effect that purpose.[72]

The British Commission on Assisted Dying, chaired by Baron Charles Falconer, concluded in 2012 that the 1961 Suicide Act should be amended to allow assistance for individuals over the age of 18, terminally ill, without medical impairment, and judged to have less than 12 months to live who have made a voluntary choice to end their lives. The government indicated its unwillingness to sponsor this legislative change.[73] Subsequently, in February, 2013, Baron Falconer introduced a Private Member's Bill to the House of Lords which—if enacted—would decriminalize the act of assisted suicide and thereby allow a terminally ill patient to receive assistance in self-administering medication to end his life or in traveling to a jurisdiction outside the U.K. to achieve that purpose.[74]

DOI: 10.1057/9781137377395

Any policy which might well emerge from analysis of a right of rational self-determination and thus, individual best interests, is also linked—inextricably—to the responsibility of the medical profession to minimize suffering—with the true extent being defined by each patient. The doctrine of medical futility would have to be re-shaped in order to accommodate assistance at this level since chronic mental illness is simply viewed today as totally different from a medical condition diagnosed as futile which results in death.[75]

Two other concerns are uppermost in any re-evaluation of the feasibility of re-defining the use and limits of palliative care for non-terminal psychological distress: the likelihood of cure from the mental illness and the competence of a mentally imbalanced patient to make a rational decision to seek humane assistance in hastening death.[76] While agreements on time frames of affliction for the full range of mental illnesses might be helpful in shaping contemporary clinical epidemiologies for use in determining non-terminal psychiatric illness that would qualify for terminal assistance, it remains arguable whether a patient diagnosed with a serious mental illness or, for example, having intermittent psychotic episodes, could ever be considered sufficiently competent to make a decision to hasten death. If new humane protocols to address the needs of those suffering from chronic psychotic distress are not forthcoming, those afflicted with mental illness will remain condemned to a form of incarceration for life where there is no palliative care.[77]

In the final analysis, the determinative question to be posited is "not whether unbearable suffering is ever a justification for suicide but whether it can ever justify the provision of assistance for someone else who might not be able to bring it of unaided."[78] The bulwark of valid normative action must be seen as being anchored to the principle of compassion.

Notes

1　SOREN KIERKEGAARD, FEAR AND TREMBLING (1843), THE SICKNESS UNTO DEATH (1849).
2　*See* ELAINE SCARRY, THE BODY IN PAIN 12 (1985); FRANCOISE BARBE-GALL, HOW TO LOOK AT A PAINTING 239–45 (2010).
3　MARK 14:34.

DOI: 10.1057/9781137377395

And, Luke records Jesus, prior to his crucifixion, expressing his anxiety and distress of what he knows is to be his future, when he asks, "Father, if thou be willing, remove this cup from me; nevertheless, not my will, but thine be done." LUKE 22:42.

4   Arthur G. Lipman, *The Scream by Edvard Munch: A Profound Portrayal of Existential Pain*, 19 J. PAIN and PALLIATIVE CARE PHARMACOTHERAPY 1 (2005).
    See generally REINHOLD HELLER, THE SCREAM (1973).

5   HELLER, *id.* at 90.

6   SCARRY, *supra* note 2 at 2.
    In the practice of medicine, pain—of which there are 58 types—is defined as "an unpleasant sensory and emotional experience arising from actual or potential tissue damage or described in terms of such damage." TABER'S CYCLOPEDIC MEDICAL DICTIONARY 1487, 1487–91 (19th ed. 2001). Psychogenic pain is used to describe mental—as opposed to pain of an organic nature. *Id.* 1491. Suffering, being subjective, cannot be measured but must be referenced to the whole person. Accordingly, suffering is defined as a "state of severe distress associated with events that threaten the intactness of [the] person." ERIC J. CASSELL, THE NATURE OF SUFFERING AND THE GOALS OF MEDICINE, 276, 312 (2nd ed. 2004). Pain affects the body and is more properly addressed by physicians. Yet, a shared responsibility exists between physicians and other caregivers to control both the pain and suffering of those who are dying. Eric J. Cassell, *The Nature of Suffering and The Goals of Medicine*, 306 NEW ENG. J. MED. 639 (Mar. 18, 1982).

7   Gunderman, *supra* Ch. 1, note 84 at 40, 43.

8   Gunderman, *id.*

9   Lois L. Shepherd, *Sophie's Choice: Medical and Legal Responses to Suffering*, 72 NOTRE DAME L. REV. 103, 146 (1996).
    See Evan D. Anderson and Correy S. Davis, *Breaking the Cycle of Preventable Suffering: Fulfilling the Principles of Balance*, 24 TEMP. INT'L & COMP. L. J. 329 (2010).

10 Shepherd, *id.* at 138.

11 CASSELL, *supra* note 6 at 291.
    See Campbell and Cox, *supra* Ch. 1, note 51.

12 Peter Strang, et al., *Existential Pain—an Entity, or Provocation, or a Challenge?*, 27 J. PAIN SYMPTOM MGT. 241 (Mar. 2004).

13 Strang et al., *id.*

14 Cicely Saunders, *Hospice*, 1 MORTALITY 317 (1996).

15 *Id.* at 320.
    For a free app and website which presents international news, commentary and analysis on hospice, Palliative and end-of-life care *see* www.ehospice. com.

DOI: 10.1057/9781137377395

16 *See* HOSPICE: THE LIVING IDEA, Ch. 8 (Cicely Saunders, et al.,eds. 1981).

17 *Id.*
    See PALLIATIVE CARE: TRANSFORMING THE CARE OF SERIOUS
    ILLNESS (Diane E. Meier et al., eds. 2010).

18 HOSPICE CARE ON THE INTERNATIONAL SCENE at 11 (Cicely
    Saunders and Robert Kastenbaum eds. 1997).

19 *Id.* at 7.
    See GLENNYS HOWARTH, DEATH AND DYING: SOCIOLOGICAL
    INTRODUCTION, Ch. 7 (2007).

20 World Health Organization (WHO), *http://www.who.int/cancer/palliative/en/*.
    See also Jan Stjernsward, Ch. 2, *The International Hospice Movement from The
    Perspective of The World Health Organization* in HOSPICE CARE ON THE
    INTERNATIONAL SCENE (Cicely Saunders and Robert Kastenbaum eds.
    1997).

21 Helene Stacks, et al., *Why Now? Timing and Circumstances of Hastened Death*,
    30 J. PAIN & SYMPTOM MGT. 215, 225 (Sept. 2005); Martin J. Fegg, et al.,
    Personal Values and Individual Quality of Life in Palliative Care Patients, 30 J.
    PAIN & SYMPTOM MGT. 154 (Aug. 2005).

22 Leon R. Kass, *Lingering Longer: Who Will Care?*, WASH. POST, Sept. 29, 2005,
    at A23.

23 Lynn, *supra* Ch. 1, note 88 at 12.

24 *Id.*
    See Len Doyal, *Dignity in Dying Should Include the Legalization of Non-
    Voluntary Euthanasia*, 1 CLINICAL ETHICS 65 (2006) (arguing under a best
    interests test, that it is beneficial and compassionate to end the suffering of
    incompetent patients experiencing intractable physical and/or emotional
    suffering from terminal illness with abbreviated life expectancy and unable
    to either conceptualize or, for that matter, demand assistance in ending life).
    See also Nigel Bunyan, *I Helped Patients die, Says Murder Case G.P.*, THE
    DAILY TELEGRAPH, June 19, 2010, at 1 (reporting on a 75 year old
    physician, Dr. Harold Martin, who admitted hastening the death of 3
    patients—for whom he had been charged with murder and was acquitted
    subsequently; he also admitted later that he had given fatal doses of
    painkillers to elderly and terminally ill patients, and in two cases without
    patient consent, acting as such, out of "Christian compassion" to limit
    suffering).
    See generally DAVID B. MORRIS, THE CULTURE OF DEATH (1991).

25 *See* Bernard Lo and Gordon Rubenfeld, *Palliative Sedation to Dying Patients:
    We Turn to it When Everything Else Hasn't Worked*, 294 JAMA 1810, 1811 (Oct.
    12, 2005); Paul Rousseau, *Existential Suffering and Palliative Sedation: A Brief
    Commentary with a Proposal for Clinical Guidelines*, 18 AM. J. HOSPICE &
    PALLIATIVE CARE 151–52 (May–June 2001).

DOI: 10.1057/9781137377395

26   Norman L. Cantor and George C. Thomas, III, *The Legal Bounds of Physician Conduct Hastening Death* 48 BUFF. L. REV. 83, 139 (2000).

27   Glenys Williams, *The Principle of Double Effect and Terminal Sedation*, 9 MEDICAL L. REV. 41–2 (2001).

28   *See generally* THOMAS A. CAVANAUGH, DOUBLE-EFFECT REASONING: DOING GOOD AND AVOIDING EVIL (2006); Norman L. Cantor, *Twenty-five Years After Quinlan: A Review of the Jurisprudence of Death and Dying* 29 J. L. MED. & ETHICS 182 (2001).

29   Victor Cellarius, *Terminal Sedation and The Imminence Condition*, 34 J. MED. ETHICS 69 (2008).

30   Joseph M. Boyle, Jr., *Toward Understanding The Principle of Double Effect*, 90 ETHICS 527 (1980).

31   *See* Report of The Council on Ethical and Judicial Affairs, *Sedation to Unconsciousness in End-of-Life Care*, CEJA Report 5-A-08 (2008).

32   *See infra* notes 49–50 and accompanying text.
     It is within the last two years of life that most medicine is used for Americans with chronic illness (diabetes, cancer, heart disease) who require hospital care. Robert Pear, *Researchers Find Huge Variations in End-of-Life Treatment*, N.Y. TIMES, April 7, 2008, at 17. As a consequence of this statistic, almost a third of Medicare monies expended go to patients in their last two years. Evan Thomas, *supra* Ch. 1, note 36.

33   Rob McStay, *Terminal Sedation: Palliative Care for Intractable Pain, Post Glucksberg and Quill*, 29 AM. J. LAW & MED. 45 (2003).

34   George P. Smith, II, *All's Well That Ends Well: Toward a Policy of Assisted Rational Suicide or Merely Enlightened Self-Determination?*, 22 U. CAL. DAVIS L. REV. 275, 283, 418–19 (1989).
     Indeed, the terms "palliative sedation," "continuous deep sedation," and "primary deep continuous sedation," are all used interchangeably, with terminal sedation and are seen as euphemisms which mask the reality of finality which is inherent when terminal sedation is administered. "Death over days" is seen as feeling "more natural" than physician-assisted suicide. Margaret P. Battin, *Terminal Sedation: Pulling the Sheet Over Our Eyes*, 38 HASTINGS CENTER RPT. 27–8 (2008). Once a terminal prognosis has been given, a concern that arises as to whether sedation should be administered within hours or days of death. There is no standard time-frame protocol. If sedation is administered within two weeks or less, typically the patient dies from underlying disease rather than the sedation. Jeffrey T. Berger, *infra* note 75.
     See generally George P. Smith, II, *Euphemistic Codes and Tell-Tale Hearts: Humane Assistance in End-of-Life Cases*, 10 HEALTH MATRIX, J. 175 (2000).

35   *See* Timothy E. Quill, Bernard Lo and Dan W. Brock, *Palliative Options of Last Resort: A Comparison of Voluntarily Stopping Eating and Drinking, Terminal*

DOI: 10.1057/9781137377395

Sedation, Physician-Assisted Suicide, and *Voluntary Active Euthanasia,* 278 JAMA 2009, 2104 (1997).

In 2008, the Council on Ethical and Judicial Affairs of the American Medical Association issued a report entitled, *"Sedation to Unconsciousness in End-of-Life Cases,"* which was hoped would bring clarity to this area of concern. CEJA Report 5-A-08, *supra* note 31. Many of the Council's conclusions have been termed "naive." *See* Battin, *supra* note 34; Kaasa and Loge, *supra* note 17, Ch. 1.

36   Quill et al., *id.* at 2103.

37   *Id.*

Elucidating on what he terms, "the last options," for dealing with refractory pain not managed effectively by traditional palliative care, Dr. Quill makes pointed observations: aggressive pain management achieved by the use of opiates, proportional to their need to manage pain, is valid—even though there is an awareness (without purposeful intent) that death will be hastened; withdrawing or withholding of life-sustaining therapies is a legal right for a competent patient to exercise; a voluntary decision by such a competent patient to cease nutrition and hydration is a valid treatment option but be an informed division to the degree that the patient understands the act of dying may take up to two weeks and physician support is essential; finally, in rare cases where none of these three medical options are considered reasonable, a disproportionate use of a sedative may be allowed to induce unconsciousness and abate pain. Timothy E. Quill, *Physician-Assisted Death in the United States: Are the Existing 'Last Resorts' Enough?,* 38 HASTINGS CENTER RPT. 17 (Sept.—Oct. 2008). While reliable statistics on the use of these options are difficult to obtain and validate, one source sets the use of sedation to unconsciousness anywhere from no deaths, less than one percent, to half of all deaths. *Id.* at 20.

38   ORE. REV. STAT. ANN. §127.800 et seq. (2003).

39   REV. CODE WASH. ANN. Ch. 70, 245 (2009).

The Supreme Court of Montana ruled on December 31, 2009, that—under the Rights of The Terminally Ill Act (MT. CODE ANN. §§ 50-9-101 to -206 1991)—competent, terminally ill patients can request physician assistance in obtaining a prescription for a lethal dose of medicine to be self-administered; and further the Act shields physicians from civil or criminal liability for any such acts of assistance. *See* Baxter v. Montana, DA 09-0051, 2009 MT. 449. Vermont enacted death with dignity legislation in May, 2013. *See* Ch. 1, *supra* note 52.

40   Quill et al., *supra* note 35 at 2103; REV. CODE WASH. ANN. Ch. 70, 245 (2009).

But see Susan R. Martyn and Henry J. Bourguigon, *Physician-Assisted Suicide: The Lethal Flaws of the Ninth and Second Circuit Decisions* 85 CAL. L. REV. 371,

DOI: 10.1057/9781137377395

405 (1997) (questioning whether deep, or terminal, sedation is the same as physician-assisted suicide).

See generally DEREK HUMPHRY, TREAD CAREFULLY WHEN YOU HELP TO DIE: ASSISTED SUICIDE AROUND THE WORLD (2005). Available at http://www.assistedsuicide .org/suicide_laws.html.

See also the comprehensive website of the Death with Dignity National Center which covers state legislative activities in assistance with the death of terminally ill patients.

41   Quill et al., *supra* note 35 at 2104.
Voluntary euthanasia occurs in those cases where a clearly competent person makes a voluntary and enduring request to be helped to end his life. STANFORD ENCYCLOPEDIA OF PHILOSOPHY. *See* http://plato. standford.edu/entries/euthanasia-voluntary/.

42   *Id.*
See generally ROGER S. MAGNUSSON, ANGELS OF DEATH: EXPLAINING THE EUTHANASIA UNDERGROUND (2002).

See Russel D. Ogden, *Non-Physician Assisted Suicide: The Technological Imperative of The Deathing Counterculture* 25 DEATH STUDIES 387 (2001) (discussing the "technological imperative" has been embraced by those wishing a quickly induced and painless death).

See also Manuel Roig-Franzi, *The End is Near*, WASH. POST MAG. 6 (Jan. 22, 2012) (discussing how plastic super market "turkey bags" provide tents for helium to be streamed into these so-called "exit hoods" and the problems arising there from together with the administration of a voluntary organization named the Final Exit Network which assists those wishing to commit suicide); PHILIP NITSCHKE, THE PEACEFUL PILL HANDBOOK (2007) (evaluating options available to those wishing to end their lives—including a drug called, Nembutal, available from Mexico, carbon monoxide, various prescription drugs and making suggestions for concealing evidence of suicide).

43   Washington v. Glucksberg, 521 U.S. 702, 710 (1997).

44   McStay, *supra* note 33 at 60.
But see Robert A. Burt, *The Supreme Court Speaks—Not Assisted Suicide but a Constitutional Right to Palliative Care*, 337 NEW ENG. J. MED. 1234 (1997).

45   McStay, *supra* note 33 at 60.
See Vacco v. Quill, 521 U.S. 793 (1997); George P. Smith, II, MONOGRAPH, Final Exits: Safeguarding Self-Determination and The Right to be Free from Cruel and Unusual Punishment (1997); George J. Annas, *The Bell Tolls for a Constitutional Right to Physician-Assisted Suicide*, 33 NEW ENG. J. MED. 1098, 1102 (Oct. 9, 1997) (observing that five members of the Vacco Court "seem to think there is something akin to a 'right not to suffer' at least when death is imminent," and when palliative care is provided by physicians whose primary intention is to relieve suffering).

DOI: 10.1057/9781137377395

46 Cruzan v. Dir., Missouri Dept. of Health, 497 U.S. 261 at 286–87.
    See also McStay, *supra* note 33 at 49.
    The Supreme Court has not given clear criteria for deciding when a right
    qualifies as a liberty interest. Accordingly, the right to die with assistance is
    best decided by state legislatures, prosecutors' offices, hospitals and private
    homes; for it is within these fora that the right is best tested and, when
    needed, acknowledged as legitimate. It should be remembered that even
    though there may be no constitutional foundation for a right to commit an
    act, this—alone—does not mean that, morally, the act is itself improper. Cass
    Sunstein, *The Right to Die*, 106 YALE L. J. 1123, 1156–57 (1997).

47 George P. Smith, II, *Utility and The Doctrine of Medical Futility: Safeguarding
    The Prohibition Against Cruel and Unusual Punishment*, 12 J. CONTEMP.
    HEALTH LAW & POL'Y 1 (1996).

48 *See* LYNN, *supra* note 23 at 12.

49 Timothy E. Quill and Ira R. Byock, *Responding to Intractable Terminal
    Suffering: The Role of Terminal Sedation and Voluntary Refusal of Food and
    Fluids*, 132 ANNALS INTERN. MED. 408, 413 (Mar. 7, 2000).
    See Maria Cheng, et al., *infra* note 56.

50 DEREK HUMPHRY, FINAL EXITS 134 (1991).

51 Quill, et al., *supra* note 49.

52 *See* Quill, et al., *supra* note 35 at n's 1, 5, 7.
    See also Editorial, *Attending to Psychological Symptom and Palliative Care*, 20 J.
    CLINICAL ONCOLOGY 624 (Feb. 2001) (concluding more than one-third
    of dying patients are depressed).

53 *See* McStay, *supra* note 33; Quill, et al., *supra* note 35.
    See also Lynn A. Jansen and Daniel P. Sulmasy, *Sedation, Alimentation,
    Hydration, and Equivocation: Careful Conversation about Care at the End of Life*,
    136 ANNALS INTERN. MED. 845 (2002).

54 *See* Albert R. Jonsen, *A History of Bioethics and Discipline and Discourse* in
    BIOETHICS: AN INTRODUCTION TO THE HISTORY, METHODS &
    PRACTICE 3–22 (Nancy C. Jecker, et al., eds. 2007).
    See also John Fletcher, *Love is The Only Measure*, 83 COMMONWEALTH 427
    (1966); JOHN FLETCHER, SITUATION ETHICS: THE NEW MORALITY
    (1966).

55 THOMASMA and GRABER, *supra* Ch. 1, note 70 at 192 *passim* (1991).

56 McStay, *supra* note 33 at 46.
    See supra Sachs, Ch. 1 at note 7.
    On March 12, 2012, the England and Wales High Court (Queen's Bench
    Division), held a paralyzed and mute—although mentally competent—
    former rugby player, Tony Nicklinson, would be granted a request to obtain a
    hearing before the High Court on the issue of whether a physician who, with
    consent, ends Nicklinson's life, can be charged with murder. Consistent with

DOI: 10.1057/9781137377395

Art. 8 of the European Convention on Human Rights, Nicklinson argues that being allowed to choose the manner in which he dies is within his basic right to a autonomous life. Tony Nicklinson v. Ministry of Justice [2012] EWHC 304. This case is momentous because it places before a judicial body the question of whether a change in the law of murder can be effected by a court of law rather than by Parliament. Maria Cheng, *British Court: Right-to-Die Can Proceed*, WASH. EXAMINER, Mar. 13, 2012, at 17. *See also* http://www.bbc.co.uk/news/uk-17336774, March 13, 2012.

This case by Nicklinson was dismissed by Britain's High Court in August, 2012, thus precluding his request to have the country's euthanasia law overturned. While concluding that any change in the present law here was a parliamentary matter, the Crown Prosecutor has said—previously—those who assisted loved ones commit suicide would not necessarily be charged with murder. Associated Press, *Euthanasia bid rejected in Britain*, WASH. POST, Aug. 17, 2012. Nicklinson died on August 22, 2012, from pneumonia after refusing nutrition and hydration.

57 THOMASMA and GRABER, *supra* Ch. 1, note 70 at 129.
Adjusted care is care adjusted, or suitable, to the progression of a medical condition. Thus, palliative care would come at the end-stage of a terminal illness while curative and rehabilitative care would be primary care at the onset of illness. *See* Sidney Wanzer, Daniel Federman et al., *The Physician's Responsibility Toward Hopelessly Ill Patients: A Second Look*, 320 NEW ENG. J. MED. 844 (Mar. 30, 1989); M. Sapir, *The Spectrum of Medical Care: Curative, Rehabilitative and Palliative*, 279 JAMA 20 (1998).
Continually adjusted care is essential to a compassionate and common sense approach to the management of pain and suffering often encountered in the dying process. Care of this nature always strikes a balance in favor of pain relief—even though a potential exists for hastening death—rather than the mere prolongation of life which is in its end-stage. THOMASMA and GRABER, *id.* at 129.

58 *Smith, supra* note 47.
See generally Lauren Shaiova, *Case Presentation: "Terminal Sedation" and Existential Distress*, 16 J. PAIN & SYMPTOM MGT. 463 (Dec. 1998).

59 *See* MARY WARNOCK and ELISABETH MacDONALD, EASEFUL DEATH: IS THERE A CASE FOR ASSISTED DYING? Ch. 3 (2008); JOHN GRIFFITHS, et al., EUTHANASIA AND LAW IN EUROPE 45 *passim* (2008); Herman Nys, *Physician Involvement in a Patient's Death: A Continental European Perspective* in READINGS IN COMPARATIVE HEALTH LAW AND BIOETHICS at 279–307 (Timothy S. Jost ed., 2nd ed., 2007).
In cases of advanced or end-stage dementia, the prognosis should be properly seen as terminal and, thus, treated only with palliative care. Sachs, *supra* Ch.1 at note 7.

DOI: 10.1057/9781137377395

60 GRIFFITHS et al., *id.*, at 51 *passim*, 275 *passim*.
The euthanized death of 45-year-old twins in Antwerp, Belgium, because they were anguished over the realization that they were going blind (but were not terminally ill)—and would be unable to see and relate to one another, has caused a new debate in the national parliament as it considers whether the present laws regulating euthanasia should be amended to include all terminally ill children and to individuals with dementia. Karen Wells, *Death of twin brothers fuels debate*, http://www.cbc.ca/news/world/story/2013/05/02/f-euthanasia-belgium-debate-sunday-edit...

In 2009, recent statistics showed that the number of people in Holland electing euthanasia was 2,636, or a 13% increase from 2,331 cases reported in 2008. Simon Caldwell, *Euthanasia Deaths on The Rise in Holland*, THE SUNDAY TELEGRAPH, June 20, 2010, at 17.

61 Jacob M. Appel, *A Suicide Right for the Mentally Ill: A Swiss Case Opens the Debate*, 37 HASTINGS CENTER RPT. 21 (May—June, 2007).

62 *Id.*
See GUENTHER LEWY, ASSISTED DEATH IN EUROPE AND AMERICA (2011); Nikola Biller-Andorno, *Physician-Assisted Suicide Should Be Permitted*, 368 NEW ENG. J. MED. 1451–52 (April 11, 203); Joachim Cohen et al., *European Public Acceptance of Euthanasia: Socio-demographic and Cultural Factors Assisted with the Acceptance of Euthanasia in 33 European Countries*, 63 SOCIAL SCIENCE & MED. 743 (2006).

63 Appel, *supra* note 61 at f.n. 4.
An elder Swiss citizen, who had no critical (*e.g.*, terminal) illness, but felt that her quality of life was marginal, was denied medical drug assistance by the Swiss courts, to commit suicide. In an appeal to the European Court of Human Rights arguing that her Article 8 rights to private and family life in the European Convention on Human Rights had been abridged, the European Court of Human Rights ruled that the Swiss Academy of Medical Sciences' guidelines for the administration of lethal drugs for those suffering critical illness were too vague and, thus, the appellants human rights had been violated. Gross v. Switzerland [2013] ECHR 429.
See Isabel McArdle, *Assisted dying in Switzerland: Under lethal drugs prescribing guidelines breached human rights*, http://ukhumanrightsblotg.com/2013/05/15/assisted-in-switzerland-unclear-lethal-dru...
See also THE GLOBALIZATION OF HEALTH CARE: LEGAL AND ETHICAL ISSUES at 166–67, 180 (I. Glenn Cohen ed. 2013).

64 MARGARET OTLOWSKI, VOLUNTARY EUTHANASIA AND THE COMMON LAW 408–09 (1997).
But see Dick L. Willems et al., *Attitudes and Practices Concerning the End of Life: A Comparison Between Physicians from The United States and from The Netherlands*, 160 ARCH. INTERN. MED. 63 (2000) (reporting on the

DOI: 10.1057/9781137377395

levels of agreement for increasing morphine for terminally ill patients and disagreement on the role of physicians to directly support euthanasia).

65   OTLOWSKI *id.* at 63.

66   Astrid Zweymert, *British Parliament Blocks Assisted Suicide Law*, http://o. reuters.com/news Article.jhtml?type=healthNews&storyID=12190846&src= r…(accessed May 16, 2006).
      See Lords Hansard, column 1221, http://www.publications/parliament.uk/pa/ ID19900/ Idhansrd/pdvn/Ids06/text/60512–2…(accessed May 12, 2006).

67   ORE. REV. STAT. ANN., § 127.800 et seq. (2003).

68   The Policy Guidelines may be found, in their entirety, at: http://www.cps.gov /uk/publications /prosecution/assisted_suicide_policy.html. An analysis of the guidelines and the extent of their application can be found in Suzanne Ost, *The De-Medicalisation of Assisted Dying: Is a Less Medicalised Model The Way Forward?* 18 MEDICAL L. REV. 497, 510–12 (2010).

69   Martin Beckford, *'Dr. Death' Ruled Too Old for Face Trial*, THE DAILY TELEGRAPH, June 26, 2010, at 4.
      See also Martin Beckford, *What the Law Says: Guidelines after The Purdy Case*, THE DAILY TELEGRAPH, June 26, 2010, at 4; Aidan O'Neill, *Assisted Suicide in the U.K.: From Crime to Right?* 40 HASTINGS CENTER RPT. (Inside back cover, unpaginated) (May—June, 2010); Cohen, *supra* note 63 at 161–70, 180.

70   Local Authority v. Z., EWHC 2817 (Fam.), as analyzed in KERRIDGE, et al., ETHICS AND LAW FOR THE HEALTH PROFESSIONS at 655–56 (3rd ed. 2009). *See also* Meisel et al., *infra* Ch. 5 at note 8 for the same prosecutorial sentiment in America; I. Glen Cohen, *Circumvention Tourism*, 97 CORNELL L. REV. 1309, 1386–90 (2012) (surveying cases where the home and the destination country differ on questions of criminal liability for assisting suicide and concluding that if the home country's motivation for criminalizing assistance is patient protection, then, it is proper to extend criminalization to circumvention tourists).

71   KERRIDGE, *id.*

72   Suzanne Ost, *The De-Medicalization of Assisted Dying: Is a Less Medicalized Model The Way Forward?* 18 MEDICAL L. REV. 497 515–17, 533 (2010).

73   *See* http://www.bbc.co.uk/news/health-16410118.
      See also Dana M. Cohen, *Looking for a Way Out: How to Escape the Assisted Suicide Law in England*, 24 EMORY INT'L L. REV. 697 (2010).
      But see the High Court of Ireland's recent decision upholding the constitutionality of the present prohibition on assisted suicide as a valid means of protecting the vulnerable members of society (*e.g.,* the old and the ill), Fleming v. Ireland and Ors, (2013) 1 EHC 2 (Jan. 10, 2013).
      On April 29, 2013, the Irish Supreme Court upheld the decision of the High Court in Fleming v. Ireland which had the effect of denying the appellant,

Marie Fleming—a terminally ill woman in the final stages of multiple sclerosis—a legally protected right to assistance in ending her life. Douglas Dalby, *Irish Woman Loses Appeal for Assisted Death.* N.Y. TIMES, April 30, 2013, at A5.

74   74   74. Rosemary Bennett, *Peer makes new bid to change law on assisted dying*, THE TIMES, Feb. 1, 2013, at 17.

75   Appel, *supra* note 61.

While there is presently no consensus for palliative sedation to unconsciousness (PSU) when there is a primary level of existential suffering, it has been suggested by one physician that where "severe existential pain" is exhibited "for which all available and reasonable effective treatments are unacceptable to the patient." PSU should be recognized as a valid medical option. Jeffrey T. Berger, *Rethinking Guidelines for The Use of Palliative Sedation*, 40 HASTINGS CENTER RPT. 32 (May—June, 2010).

Another highly contentious procedure is Early Terminal Sedation (ETS) which is administered before there is, clinically, active dying. Its validation and use involve combining two distinct treatment decisions: the right to refuse nutrition and hydration and to receive palliative sedation. The difference between ETS and Terminal Sedation (TS) is that the former involves combining a cessation of nutrition and hydration in patients *capable* of receiving both either orally or paternally with continuous sedation while TS involves cases where the sedation is administered to those for whom such acts of nutrition and hydration no longer sustain life. Victor Cellarius, *Early Terminal Sedation as a Distinct Entity*, 25 BIOETHICS 47 (2011).

76   Appel, *supra* note 61.

Additional concerns in determining the competency of an individual to make rational decisions of this nature would include whether consideration of this "final" alternative is of an impulsive nature and made without coercion; and whether the decision is congruent with the actual personal values of the distressed patient. JAMES L. WERTH, JR., RATIONAL SUICIDE? IMPLICATIONS FOR MENTAL HEALTH PROFESSIONALS 63–5 (1996).

77   WARNOCK and MacDONALD, *supra* note 59 at 33, 34.

78   *Id.* at 30.

See THOMASMA and GRABER, *supra* note Ch. 1, note 70 at 193 (arguing that there should be a level of social responsibility to aid those enduring pain and suffering at death).

Being an Alzheimer disease patient does not preclude that individual from being recognized, legally, as competent to make health care decisions regarding treatment or non treatment if the decision-making is undertaken in the early onset stage of the disease before recognition is lost. ALLEN E. BUCHANAN and DON W. BROCK, DECIDING FOR OTHERS: THE

DOI: 10.1057/9781137377395

ETHICS OF SURROGATE DECISION MAKING 281 (1989); George P. Smith, II, *Reviving the Swan Extending the Curse of Methuselah or Adhering to the Kervorkian Ethic?*, 2 CAMBRIDGE Q. HEALTHCARE ETHICS 49, 51 (1993); Rosemary Bennett, *Aided suicide 'will increasingly be choice of dementia patients,'* THE TIMES, May 31, 2013, at 12.

DOI: 10.1057/9781137377395

3

Medical Futility: The Template for Decisionmaking

Abstract: *This chapter studies and advocates the principle of medical futility as a template for assessing whether a medical condition is curative, rehabilitative, or palliative. Physicians should have clear markers for non-treatment. Yet, not all hospital management policies regarding futility are, however, uniform. And, there is wide disagreement regarding the propriety of use this principle to afford or "license." In dealing with cases of futility, the primary goal is to achieve—for the patient—a level of "total good." This response is realized when a balance is struck between effectiveness of the response and the benefit and burden of it, as assessed co-operatively, within an alliance between the treating physician, the patient, or, by his or her surrogate decision-maker.*

George P. Smith. *Palliative Care and End-of-Life Decisions.* New York: Palgrave Macmillan, 2013.
DOI: 10.1057/9781137377395.

Quality of life, sanctity of creation or vitalism

All too frequently, when sanctity of life or vitalism is embraced as a religious or moral construct, it then becomes impervious to rational argument.[1] When juxtaposed with quality of life, the religious view complicates and, it is argued, often trumps common sense and humane policy making which favors the standard of quality of life as the more rational construct for decisionmaking in end-stage illness.[2] Instead of one principle or concern dominating the other, both should be used in evaluating a patient's medical prognosis and placing "hope"[3] for recovery within a proper, realistic context—all consistent with, as such, patient values.

While it may be acknowledged that quality of life varies from person to person and, thus, cannot be set by one uniform standard, it can be tested by a sense of compassion or mercy. If a terminal patient is suffering greatly—physically or mentally—it makes common sense that medically approved actions must be undertaken to alleviate that suffering. Failure to act accordingly is surely an affront to the very notion of human dignity. No practical purpose is served by becoming mired in ambiguous and subtle philosophical refinements which defy not only the medical principle of futility but compassion and mercy as well.[4]

Rather than analyze and "test" supposed levels of intent in the management of end-stage illness, it is reasonable to simply isolate the standard of proportionality from the "traditional" principle or test of double effect and assess the patient costs of following a course of action with the benefits from such action.[5] Accordingly, if a decision to terminate care is in proportion to the amount of "quality" remaining in a case where the patient is in a terminal condition, that decision should be recognized as not only rational but efficacious and humane. Anchored at the fulcrum of cost-benefit test of proportionality is the principle of medical futility which is supported and complemented by the principle of compassion and the cardinal principle of beneficence. If re-designed or re-calibrated as urged in this book, a new contemporary approach to managing ethical issues in end-of-life care will be effected and one that is freed of taxonomical ambiguity as is seen in the classical principle of double effect.

Clinical applications

In 1974, Richard A. McCormick, S.J., suggested a basic medical approach, consistent with the American Medical Association's 1974

DOI: 10.1057/9781137377395

policy on the issue, to determine when life is no longer meaningful.[6] For Fr. McCormick, when there is irrefutable evidence that biological death is imminent, no extraordinary measures should be undertaken to sustain life.[7] That evidence was to be tested by a state of condition for the individual patient where there is a "negation of any truly human—i.e., relational-potential" or relationships.[8]

Recognizing that this standard of relational capacity is not subject to precise mathematical deduction, Fr. McCormick urged the medical profession to agree on concrete categories or presumptive symptoms to aid in reaching this judgment.[9] When maintenance of life means the prolongation of pain, with little or no chance of a real or sustainable level of qualitative recovery or rehabilitation, there is really no opportunity to grasp or seek overall meaning of life or "relational-potential." At this point, such actions should be recognized as being futile and cease.[10]

Today, Fr. McCormick's analytical approach is absorbed within the doctrine or principle of medical futility. Although McCormick abjured quality of life indices for determining when life should be maintained or allowed to end, it is argued here that the indicia, when shaped by standards of mercy, compassion, love or humanism, are indeed to be seen as an integral part of the clinical use of medical futility.[11] Accordingly, the principle of medical futility comes into play in those clinical cases where: a cure is physiologically impossible; the treatment is non-beneficial or unlikely to be beneficial; and in those cases where treatment, while plausible, has yet to be validated.[12]

An alternative to defining futility concludes that no obligation exists to offer treatment or maintain existing treatment. Thus, when an intervention—even a life-sustaining one—which is verified by contemporary clinical experience and medical knowledge: holds no reasonable promise for effecting recovery; imposes burdensome consequences "grossly disproportionate" to any expected benefit; has no efficacious value in mitigating patient discomfort; or serves only to artificially delay death "by sustaining or restoring a vital function," no obligation exists to either offer such treatment or, for that matter, maintain it.[13]

Admitting futile treatment negates the primary obligation of health care professionals to "do no harm."[14] When a physician prescribes a modality of treatment knowing that it is futile, he is exposing—needlessly—the patient to additional risks associated with the treatment such as infection or other adverse reactions. Even if futile treatment does not affect the patient adversely, the mere exposure to risk is cruel. Moreover, some interventions—such as CPR—inflict severe physical trauma.[15]

DOI: 10.1057/9781137377395

Administering CPR when there is no medically reasonable chance that a distressed patient will recover from the underlying illness amounts to physical torture.[16] Accordingly, physicians should be under a duty not to administer futile treatments because, by doing so, they are indeed inflicting cruel and unusual punishment on their patients and their families.[17]

Dr. Edmund D. Pellegrino, former Chairman of the President's Council on Bioethics, suggests that the primary goal in dealing with cases of futility is achieving for the patient—a level of "total good." This, in turn, then, is realized when a carefully calibrated balance is struck between three criteria: effectiveness, benefit and burden reached, co-operatively, within an "alliance" between the treating physician, the patient or his surrogate decision-maker.[18] For Dr. Pellegrino, futility is not an isolated, empirical yes/no test. Rather, each judgment of futility takes all aspects of a patient's total life experience into account—physical, mental, spiritual preferences together with life goals. As such, each judgment "demands prudential assessment for a particular person in a particular experience of illness and within a particular metaphysical and theological context."[19]

Closely, if not inextricably, related to the doctrine of medical futility is the principle of proportionality. Accordingly, under this principle, there is no obligation to provide a specific treatment when overuse or underuse of it create an unreasonable burden where the harm or suffering inflicted by such treatment is disproportionate to any realistic benefit derived from it.[20] Often presented as a cost/benefit theory, the factors used—however—in specific applications to effect the balancing test under this principle are not uniformly quantified.[21] In an effort to bring structure to this contentious issue, Dr. Pellegrino suggests "disproportionate" use is—simply—medical care which, under prevailing standards of medicine, is futile.[22]

Clarifying euphemistic codes

There are but two basic responses to individuals in cardiopulmonary arrest: order-code or no code.[23] Thus, to code a patient means—in essence—to commence cardiopulmonary resuscitation (CPR). A no code—most commonly, DNR—means no aggressive assistance will be given to a patient in medical distress.[24] Many consider a CPR order to be a "bad prognostic sign" because, put simply, few code survivors leave the hospital.[25] Indeed, an in-hospital survival rate of 50% is considered quite impressive.[26] Providing CPR, for example, to patients with metastatic cancer would be considered medically futile—this, because survival after CPR is reported to be zero.[27]

When there are no orders written which specify what resuscitative measures should be taken with particular patients, hospital policies may well dictate that a full code should be called or, in other words, resuscitation be initiated.[28] Yet, circumstances may arise where it is just as appropriate to—instead of calling a code—initiate minimal resuscitative measures which do not rise to the level of being a full blown code[29] and might be termed a "short code." This type of code is sometimes referred to as a *show code* and allows the health care personnel to initiate resuscitation and then proceed to stop their actions either after a few tried or a period of time pre-determined.[30] This code is taken largely as but a symbolic gesture designed to re-assure or placate the family of a patient or the health care personnel, themselves—that "everything was done."[31]

The *show, soft, slow, partial, limited* or *light blue* codes are all termed intermediate codes. Each designation conveys pertinent information concerning not only the type but the extent of response to be followed in the event of a patient suffering cardiopulmonary arrest. Thus, a partial, limited, or soft code is taken commonly to set forth those circumstances where either drugs might be administered without chest compressions or where resuscitation is initiated but drugs or incubation would be withheld.[32]

When there are no demonstrable benefits to a medical intervention which maintains an expiring patient other than the act of survival itself, the best interests of the patient may not be served by a resuscitation.[33] Accordingly, in those cases where a physician—more likely a reside, but occasionally an attending—is convinced of the futility or potential harm of further treatment, an intermediate code may be negotiated. This action may well have the effect of over-riding the wishes of the patient, family or even private or attending physicians but allows the resident physician a convoluted way to avoid hospital policies. Stated otherwise, such a course of action, "allowed them a means of restricting their therapeutic activity when they confronted the possibility of having to provide treatment they not only thought was futile but could also inflict significant harm on the patient."[34] The intermediate or limited code has the ultimate effect, then, of providing a means by which resident hospital physicians guard themselves not only against in-house disciplinary action and legal liability but control as well the extent to which they are forced to pursue

DOI: 10.1057/9781137377395

futile drains of their time and hospital resources.[35] It is an artful euphemism, to be sure.

As observed, the testing and application of the standard of medical futility should be tied to individual patient or goals.[36] Yet, practice has shown that physicians fail to discuss CPR with their adult patients who are admitted for medical and surgical care.[37] Indeed, a fuller discussion of DNRs with AIDS and cancer patients is harder than with patients without diseases with poor prognosis (e.g., coronary artery, and cirrhosis).[38]

The Federal Patient Self-Determination Act (PSDA) enacted in 1990[39] was designed to facilitate a full exchange of health care information when a patient is admitted to either Medicare or Medicaid-funded hospitals, skilled nursing home facilities, or home health agencies and hospitals.[40] Specifically, this law requires that all pertinent state laws concerning advance directives be disclosed.[41] Patients are accepted for care regardless of whether they fail to execute advance directives.[42]

Failure to execute an advance health care directive, for whatever reason (e.g., illiteracy, reluctance to confront death),[43] quite often presents a perplexing situation for hospice care providers. While the undergirding principle of hospice philosophy is not to postpone death,[44] when a hospice patient goes into cardiac arrest without an advance directive detailing what course of medical action (treatment or non-treatment) is desired, the hospice provider is normally obligated to attempt CPR on that patient.[45]

The obvious professional conflict in a scenario of this type is that there is a medical recognition that CPR performed on hospice patients is simply futile and runs counter to, as observed, the whole philosophy of hospice care: not to forestall death.[46] This befuddled state of affairs is best remedied by either amending the Federal Patient Self-Determination Act to allow hospice physicians to exercise their medical judgments in the "best interests" of their patients when cardiac arrest is experienced or—alternatively—promulgate a new regulation under the Medicare Hospice Benefits scheme to allow action of this nature when deemed reasonable.[47]

Two states, Georgia[48] and New York,[49] have been leaders in codifying CPR procedures. New York states the presumption that every person admitted to a hospital consents to CPR when presented with cardiac or respiratory arrest—unless there is a consent to the issuance of an order not to resuscitate.[50] The pertinent Georgia law, interestingly, acknowledges a presumption as well—but, not that every patient shall be administered CPR. Rather, it is presumed every patient agrees to

DOI: 10.1057/9781137377395

this procedure "unless it is medically futile."[51] Obviously between these two statutory approaches, if any is to be preferred, the Georgia model is stronger because it retains the professional judgmental authority of health care providers to act in their assessment of what course of action is in the best interests of their patients under emergency circumstances.

Rather than codify, legislatively, formal procedures governing decisions not to resuscitate as Georgia[52] and New York[53] have done—even though these two laws correspond generally to the CPR guidelines published by the American Medical Association and required in accredited hospitals[54]—there is clinical evidence suggesting that the same results can be achieved through institutional policy which has the effect of making the burdensome provisions of these type of laws not only redundant but inefficient and unnecessary.[55] Institutional policies should be developed and maintained which center on the patient's (or, in the event of incompetence, their surrogate's) informed consent, as well as the education of health care workers with respect to the law.[56] These policies or guidelines must maintain a critical balance—they must set out the specific requirements for a properly issued DNR order without being so restrictive as to force physicians to return to the use of slow codes. If an institution creates or adopts a working definition of futility, it will be instrumental in its efforts to maintain this balance. Acceptance of the futility doctrine can serve, additionally, as an impetus for attaining macro economic utility in the distribution of health care resources.[57]

If the institutional guidelines are unduly restrictive or open to misinterpretation, the physicians will likely provide futile CPR. Since the administration of futile medical treatment is tantamount to inflicting cruel and unusual punishment a physician has a moral, ethical, and legal duty to prohibit such treatment.[58] Clear guidelines that recognize a patient's limited right to receive treatment combined with a working definition of futility can, then, dissuade a physician's use of slow codes. If the physician does not have to resort to covert issuance of DNR orders, he can maintain an open channel of communication to the patient.

Model legislative guidance

All too often, the clinical application of substantive medical norms to aid in decisionmaking remain under and beyond the understanding of patients, their health proxies, and their families.[59] Today, hospital

DOI: 10.1057/9781137377395

management policies regarding the determination of medical futility are grounded normally in a "consultative consensus building approach."[60] Yet, interestingly, ten states have adopted the Uniform Health Care Decision Act[61] and thereby have gone on record that there must be a point of closure or finality in end-of-life care giving where consultation must yield eventually to decisive action. Under this Act, there is no "absolute" obligation on the provider's part to honor a health care surrogate's demand for the initiation or continuation of care.[62] Any such refusal of medical care may be grounded on the determination by the attending physician that the care would be "ineffective"[63] contrary to generally accepted "health care standards"[64] or be in violation of "conscience."[65] This model legislation is a bold step forward in bringing much needed clarity and finality to an area of decisionmaking clouded inherently with emotional stress.

Sedation hastened death

When, despite aggressive efforts to control severe intractable symptoms, such as dyspnea, pain or myoclonus, vomiting, delirium, anxiety or agitation, sedating medications do not achieve success and the symptoms remain severe, the sedation for intractable distress of such a dying patient is proper.[66] There is wide disagreement, however, on the propriety of using this when the patient is suffering from psychological or emotional distress and not physical pain.[67] Yet, it is the position of this book that instead of separating the somatic from the non-somatic in assessing and evaluating a course of proper medical treatment for end-stage illness, charity should be the "final principle and ultimate virtue of care for the dying."[68] And, the extent or degree of charity or compassion shown—from a standard of health care delivery and law—should, in turn, be framed by the doctrine of medical futility[69] or adjusted care.[70] To continue treatment which is medically futile would be morally wrong; for it "would deny the fact of human finitude and impose unnecessary effort, expense, and emotional trauma on the patient and on others."[71] Indeed, to continue treatment of futile medical conditions can be understood as violating the primary principle of traditional medical ethics: beneficence.[72]

Autonomous patients may request sedation in order to abate severe distress manifested by unrelieved pain, restlessness or mental anguish.

DOI: 10.1057/9781137377395

Here, the intent of the physician administering the sedation is to alleviate the distress by either "decreasing mental anguish or lessening the patient's awareness of it."[73] Often the sedation is intermittent and has been termed "respite"[74] or "twilight sleep"[75] leading to the concern by some that it is, again, but a euphemism for euthanasia—especially when the procedure is used for non-autonomous patients. Others argue that the degree or extent of sedation used is for non-autonomous patients.[76] Others argue that the degree or extent of sedation used is tied to the level of patient distress—with the sole purpose being that of alleviating the distress.[77]

Both in the case of the terminally ill autonomous patient and the non-autonomous patient suffering medical distress, even though there is a significant risk that life may well be shortened, the generally accepted policy is that when all other "traditional" efforts at pain management are ineffective, "…the great benefits of alleviating such suffering by sedation…outweigh the harm entailed in the risk of shortening life."[78] The logic of this policy is found—very directly—in a straightforward application of cost/benefit analysis.[79]

A protocol for palliative sedation of existential pain

In order for palliative or "terminal sedation" to be administered, patients presenting should: be diagnosed as being terminally ill[80]—or moribund;[81]—had a current Do Not Resuscitate order listed in their medical records; have exhausted all palliative treatments for anxiety, delirium or depression;[82] received a psychological evaluation by a qualified clinician together with a similar assessment of spiritual issues, which may be particular to the needs of a patient, by either a member of the clergy or other qualified clinician;[83] participate in a candid discussion with their physician and/or family regarding the costs versus the benefits of a course of palliative sedation; and, subsequent to this discussion, an informed consent to the therapy should be obtained, again, from the patient or his surrogate decision-maker; finally, consideration should be given to whether a trial of respite sedation should first be undertaken before the deep sedation.[84] With respite sedation, a sedative is ordered for a pre-determined time frame—for example 24 to 48 hours, with a

DOI: 10.1057/9781137377395

downward titration of the sedative occurring until the patient is restored to consciousness.[85]

The significant value to this eight-step suggested protocol is that not only may a re-assessment be made of the patient's condition by his family and health care team, but this course of action may ease or cease altogether the distress which initiated the request for continuous sedation and thereby resolve the need for additional sedation. When trials of respite sedation are inconclusive or fail, all parties to the plan for full palliative sedation should be advised that death may not occur for days or even weeks.[86]

The final step in this model protocol requires a dosage policy to be established which is unequivocal and forbids increase in the level of sedative unless the patient awakens or otherwise presents evidence of suffering (e.g., restlessness, grimaces or withdraws from stimuli)[87] or discomfort (e.g., displays a furrowed brow or develops hypertension).[88] Establishing in advance of the actual sedation a classification scale could also go far toward alleviating inconsistencies of treatment. Thus, for cancer patients, "primary continuous deep sedation for delirium" could be ordered and for patients with dyspnea caused by lung cancer, "secondary continuous mild sedation" could be ordered.[89] When lower doses are ineffective to provide symptomatic relief, then—and only then—should dosages be increased.[90] To neglect the establishment of a policy of this type could well give rise to an impression or allegation that the attending physician was hastening death and had exceeded the bounds of a medically efficacious therapy in palliative sedation and thereby embrace euthanasia or physician-assisted suicide.[91]

Public misconceptions

Because, in popular conception, the administration of barbiturates has been associated with euthanasia—especially in The Netherlands—their use in the United States for palliative care treatments has been seen as something akin to unethical conduct.[92] Their use can, however, be justified easily under the principle of double effect—this, simply because their use provides effective comfort for those at the end stages of life.[93] As well, and in further justification, as suggested, a simple standard of compassion and adjusted care can serve as a guide for pharmacological use of barbiturates.

DOI: 10.1057/9781137377395

A noble effort toward clarification?

In a report of the American Medical Association's Council on Ethical and Judicial Affairs released in 2008, dealing with the subject of sedation to unconsciousness in end-of-life care,[94] a number of conclusions are reached: 1) "The use of sedation in palliative care is not ethically controversial;"[95] 2) Sedating to unconsciousness is a valid option of medical treatment for those who are "terminally ill" and have "clinical symptoms" which are "unresponsive to aggressive, symptom-specific treatments;"[96] 3) Before sedating to unconsciousness, informed consent must be obtained from the patient or the patient's designated health care surrogate;[97] 4) Consultation with a "multidisciplinary team"—including a palliative care specialist—should be undertaken in order to determine whether this form of sedation is viewed presently, based on past treatments, as "appropriate;"[98] 5) Physician–patient discussions are held which consider the plan for sedation, its length of administration (intermittent or constant) and the expectations of treatment;[99] 6) A process of implementation is co-ordinated which monitors the appropriateness of care during the sedation;[100] 7) Addressing issues of existential pain should not be deemed appropriate through the use of palliative sedation. Rather, existential suffering should be addressed "by providing the patient with needed social support;"[101] and 8) The intentional use of palliative sedation to "cause a patient's death" is never allowed.[102]

While this Report may be seen as a noble effort to clarify and even "resolve" inherent difficulties and imprecision surrounding the administration of palliative sedation, there remains a fatal flaw in the Report: that is, its continued reliance on "intention" as the paramount guide or construct for determining when opiate and sedative use is palliative and not to be seen as either euthanasia or physician-assisted suicide.[103] The Report embraces the doctrine of double effect as the tool to test whether proper intent is shown in pharmacologic therapies.[104] Although recognizing proportionality as a "central tenet of the principle of double effect," the Report[105] tries—unsuccessfully—and "naively"[106]—to gauge intent and measure proportionality by dosage uses.[107] Accordingly, when there are continuous infusions or repeated dosages, these actions may be seen as "indicators of proportionate palliative sedation."[108] Contrariwise, "one large dose or rapidly accelerating doses...may signify lack of knowledge or an inappropriate intention to hasten death."[109] An alternative explanation for repeated doses and infusions might well be that

DOI: 10.1057/9781137377395

such dosage patterns are little more than a "clever attempt to cover one's tracks."[110]

It is argued subsequently in this book that instead of miring and indeed shackling humane patient care in end-of-life cases to the ambiguous doctrine of double effect, a more efficacious test for determining the medial propriety of pharmacologic therapies should be whether their benefits, based on sound medical judgment, simply outweigh the costs of not applying the therapies.[111] A rational, common sense decisionmaking process, bereft of uncertainties and focused on what actions are beneficent and in the best interests of the terminal patient, should be determinative.[112]

Notes

1 RONALD A. LINDSAY, FUTURE BIOETHICS: OVERCOMING TABOOS, MYTHS AND DOGMAS 52 (2008).

2 *Id.*
   See ROBERT YOUNG, MEDICALLY ASSISTED DEATH Ch. 3 (2007).

3 Adrienne M. Martin, *Hope and Exploitation*, 38 HASTINGS CENTER RPT. 49 (2008).

4 Edmund D. Pellegrino, *Decision at The End of Life: The Use and Abuse of The Concept of Futility* in THE DIGNITY OF THE DYING PERSON at 231 (Juan De Dios Vial Correa and Elio Segreccia eds. 2000), Proceedings of the Fifth Assembly of The Pontifical Academy of Life, Feb., 1999.

5 *Id.* (observing disproportionate is synonymous with futility).
   See Timothy E. Quill, *Physicians Should 'Assist Suicide' When It is Appropriate*, 40 J. LAW MED ETHICS 57 (2012).

6 Richard A. McCormick, *To Save or Let Die: The Dilemma of Modern Medicine* 229 JAMA 172 (1974).

7 *Id.*

8 *Id.*
   Dr. Joseph Fletcher suggested a number of factors could be used to test whether one's medical state is consistent with common indicators of personhood. The pivotal factor is whether the at-risk patient has a functioning cortex. Joseph Fletcher, *A Tentative Profile of Man*, 2 HASTINGS CENTER RPT. 1 (Nov. 1972).

9 McCormick, *supra* note 6.

10 *Id.*

11 Smith, *supra* Ch. 2, note 47.

DOI: 10.1057/9781137377395

12   Lawrence J. Schneiderman and Nancy Jecker, *Futility in Practice*, 153 ARCH. INTERN. MED. 437, 440 (1993).

13   Lance K. Stell, *Stopping Treatment on the Grounds of Futility: A Role for Institutional Policy*, 11 ST. LOUIS U. PUB. L. REV. 481, 495 (1992).
      Any request that medical therapy be offered to patients who would have less than a 1% chance of success should be deemed unreasonable and, thus futile. Lawrence F. Schneiderman, Nancy S. Jecker and Albert R. Jonsen, *Medical Futility: Its Meaning and Ethical Implications* in BIOETHICS: AN INTRODUCTION TO THE HISTORY, METHODS AND PRACTICE at 408, 412 (Nancy S. Jecker, et al., eds. 2d 2007).

14   John L. Paris, et al., *Physician's Refusal of Requested Treatment: The Case of Baby L*, 322 NEW ENG. J. MED. 112, 1014 (1990).

15   Smith, *supra* Ch. 2, note 34.

16   *Id.*

17   Smith, MONOGRAPH, *supra* Ch. 2, note 45.

18   Pellegrino, *supra* note 4 at 227.
      See Mark A. Hall, *Law, Medicine, and Trust*, 55 STAN. L. REV. 463 (2002).

19   Pellegrino, *supra* note 4 at 240.

20   Margaret A. Somerville, *The Song of Death: The Lyrics of Euthanasia*, 9 J. CONTEMP. HEALTH LAW & POL'Y 1, 62 (1993).

21   TOM L. BEAUCHAMP and JAMES F. CHILDRESS, PRINCIPLE OF BIOMEDICAL ETHICS 228–34 (3rd ed. 1989).

22   Pellegrino, *supra* note 4 at 229.
      For medical treatments seen as "extraordinary" and excessively burdensome, the Roman Catholic Church in 1957, through Pope Pius XII, concluded such can licitly be withdrawn. Pellegrino, *id.* at 219. And, in 1980, the Declaration on Euthanasia was issued by the Sacred Congregation for the Doctrine of the Faith which sought to amplify the policy for testing when medical treatment is disproportionate to the benefit conferred by it. Pellegrino, *id.* at 229. Accordingly, the Congregation suggests the type of treatment and its complexity be compared (or balanced) against the result to be expected from its use while considering the state of the ill person, his physician, and their moral resources. *Id.*

23   Judith M. Saunders and Sharon M. Valente, *Code/No Code? The Question That Won't Go Away*, 16 NURSING 60, 62 (Mar. 1986).

24   *Id.*
      See generally Dean M. Hashimoto, *A Structural Analysis of The Physician-Patient Relationship in No-Code Decisionmaking*, 93 YALE L. J. 362 (1983).

25   Saunders and Valente, *supra* note 23 at 63.

26   *Id.*
      The Council on Ethical and Judicial Affairs of the American Medical Association has reported that in approximately one-third of some two

DOI: 10.1057/9781137377395

million patient deaths occurring in hospitals in the United States each year, CPR is attempted in approximately one-third of this population. Of those receiving CPR, one-third survive and one-third of these individuals survive, in turn, until discharged from the hospital. Ultimately, the success or failure of CPR resuscitation depends upon the nature and severity of a patient's major illness before arresting. *Guidelines for The Appropriate Use of Do Not Resuscitate to Orders*, 265 JAMA 1868, 1869 (April 10, 1991).

27 Bernard Lo, *Unanswered Questions About DNR Orders*, 265 JAMA 1874 (April 10, 1991).

28 *See* Judith W. Ross and Deborah Pugh, *Limited Cardiopulmonary Resuscitation: The Ethics of Partial Codes*, QUALITY REV. BULL. 4 (Jan. 1988).

29 Felice Quigley, *Legalities of The No Code/Slow Code*, PENNSYLVANIA NURSE 15 (Oct. 1988).

30 *Id.*

31 Jessica H. Muller, *Shades of Blue: The Negotiations of Limited Codes by Medical Residents*, 34 SOC. SCI. MED. 885, 890, 896 (1992).

32 *Id.* at 890.

33 *Id.* at 894.

34 *Id.*
    DNR orders "are commonly made without consultation with the patient," Emily Jackson, *Death, Euthanasia and the Medical Profession* in DEATH RITES AND RIGHTS, Ch. 3 at 49 (Belinda Brooks-Gordon et al., eds. 2007).

35 Muller, *supra* note 31 at 895.

36 Pellegrino, *supra* note 4.

37 Lo, *supra* note 27.

38 *Id.*

39 42 U.S.C. §§1395 cc(f), 1396 a (a) (1994) (Medicare and Medicaid respectively).
    This 1990 legislation was the basis for subsequent regulations on Advance Directives under the Patient Self-Determination Act, itself. *See* 60 FED. REG. 33, 261–33, 294 (June 27, 1996) (codified at 42 CFR Parts 417, 430, 431, 434, 483, 484, and 489).

40 *See* GEORGE P. SMITH, II, LEGAL AND HEALTHCARE ETHICS FOR THE ELDERLY Ch. 7 (1996); Laurence P. Ulrich, *The Patient Self-Determination Act: Meeting the Challenges of Patient Care*, 283 JAMA 2454 (2000).

41 *See Patient Self-Determination Act, supra* note 39.
    See generally Joseph T. Monohan and Elizabeth A. Laeoharn, *Life-Sustaining Treatment and the Law: The Evolution of Informed Consent, Advance Directives and Surrogate Decision Making*, 19 ANNALS HEALTH L. 107 (2010).

42 Lainie Rutkow, *Dying to Live: The Effort of The Patient Self Determination Act on Hospice Care*, 7 N.Y.U. J. LEGIS. & PUB. POL'Y 393, 396 (2003–04).

DOI: 10.1057/9781137377395

43 *Id.,* at 396 n's 14–16.

44 *Id.,* at 397 et al.

45 *Id.* at 396.
See N.Y. PUB. HEALTH LAW §2962 (2007).

46 Rutkow, *id.* at 435.

47 *Id.* at 434–35.

48 GA. CODE §31–39–1 et al. (Supp. 2010).

49 N.Y. PUB. HEALTH LAW §2962 et al. (2007).

50 *Id.* at §2962.
It has been argued that physicians should be liable in battery for administering life-saving treatment—not withstanding doubts about the validity of a patient's treatment refusal—unless reasonable mistake can be established. Sabine Michalowski, *Trial and Error in The End of Life—No Harm Done?*, 27 OXFORD J. LEGAL STUDIES 257 (2007).

51 GA. CODE §31–39–3 (Supp. 2010).

52 *Id.*

53 N.Y. PUB. HEALTH LAW §2962 et al. (2007).

54 Carol A. Mooney, *Deciding Not to Resuscitate Hospital Patients: Medicaid and Legislative Perspectives*, 1986 U. ILL. L. REV. 1025, 1044 (1986).

55 Russell S. Kamer and John A. Clung, *New York's Do-Not-Resuscitate Law: Burden or Benefit?* in LEGISLATING MEDICAL ETHICS: A STUDY OF THE NEW YORK DO-NOT-RESUSCITATE LAW at 230, 234 *passim* (Robert. Baker and Martin A. Strosberg eds. 1995) (using Matter of Storar, 52 N.Y. 2d 517 (1981) as an example)).

56 Smith, *supra* Ch. 2, note 47.

57 *Id.* at 36.
See generally SHARON R. KAUFMANN, … AND A TIME TO DIE: HOW AMERICAN HOSPITALS SHAPE THE END OF LIFE (2005).

58 Smith, *supra* Ch. 2, note 47 at 36.

59 One study discovered that conflicts arose in 78% of cases where issues of limiting life-sustaining medical treatment were in play and normally involved a demand of health care providers to provide care when a decision was made that such action was either inappropriate or futile. Thaddeus M. Pope and Ellen A. Wallmas, *Meditation at The End of Life: Getting Beyond The Limits of The Talking Cure*, 22 OHIO STATE J. DISPUTE RESOLUTION, 1, 4 at n. 13 (2007).

60 Sandra H. Johnson, et al., *Legal and Institutional Policy Responses to Medical Futility*, 30 J. HEALTH & HOSP. L. 21, 31 (1997).

61 Unif. Health Care Decisions Act §§ 1–19, 9 UNF. LAWS ANN. 93 (1993).

62 *Id.* Prefatory Note 7.

63 *Id.,* § 13 (d).

64 *Id.,* §§ 7(f) and 13(d).

DOI: 10.1057/9781137377395

65   *Id.*, § 7(e).

66   Eric L. Krakauer, Richard T. Penson, Robert D. Truog et al., *Sedation for Intractable Distress of a Dying Patient: Acute Palliative Care and The Principle of Double Effect*, 5 THE ONCOLOGIST 53 (2000).

67   *Id.*

68   Pellegrino, *supra* note 4 at 241.

69   *Smith, supra* Ch. 2, note 47.

70   *See* George P. Smith, II, *Terminal Sedation as Palliative Care: Revalidating a Right to a Good Death*, 7 CAMBRIDGE Q. HEALTHCARE ETHICS 382, 383 (1998).

71   Pellegrino, *supra* note 4 at 235.

72   *Id.* at 223.
     When a patient is in end-stage illness, yet not in peril of immediate death, efforts to sedate "toward death" are seen by some as unethical. *See, e.g.,* Daniel P. Sulmasy, *The Use and Abuse of The Principle of Double Effect*, 3 CLIN. PULMONARY MED. 86 (1996).

73   Timothy E. Quill and Ira R. Byock, *Responding to Intractable Terminal Suffering: The Role of Terminal Sedation and Voluntary Refusal of Food and Fluids*, 132 ANNALS OF INTERNAL MEDICINE 408, 409 (2000); Pope and Anderson, *infra* note 91.

74   Williams, *supra* Ch. 2, note 27 at 41, 49.

75   *Id.*

76   RANDALL and DOWNIE, *supra* Ch. 1, note 17 at 72.
     Another less troubling euphemism for terminal sedation is sedation hastened death.

77   *Id.*

78   *Id.*

79   *Id.*
     See also Williams *supra* note 74 at 41.

80   Paul Rousseau, *Existential Suffering and Palliative Sedation: A Brief Commentary with a Proposal for Clinical Guidelines*, 18 AM. J. HOSPICE & PALLIATIVE CARE 151, 152 (2001).

81   Bernard Lo and Gordon Rubenfeld, *Palliative Sedation in Dying Patients: 'We Turn to it When Everything Else Hasn't Worked,'* 294 JAMA 1810, 1812 (Oct. 12, 2005).

82   Rousseau, *supra* note 80 at 152.

83   *Id.* at 153.

84   *Id.* at 153.

85   *Id.*
     See Quill and Byock, *supra* note 73 at 413, Table 2, Medications Used for Terminal Sedation (2000); Cellarius, *supra* Ch. 2, note 75.

86   Rousseau, *supra* note 80 at 153.

DOI: 10.1057/9781137377395

87   *Id.*

88   Lo and Rubenfeld, *supra* note 81 at 1813.

89   Morita et al., *Definition of Sedation for Symptom Relief: A Systematic Literature Review and a Proposal for Operational Criteria*, 24 J. PAIN SYMPTOM MGT. 447, 452 (2008).

90   Lo and Rubenfeld, *supra* note 81 at 1812.

91   Rousseau, *supra* note 80 at 153.
An alternative five-step protocol for the administration of terminal sedation as palliative care requires five conditions be met before its administration: severe suffering (even though standard palliative care has been provided); no therapeutic options are seen as effective within disease prognosis; survival is severely limited; an explicit desire for sedation has been made by the at-risk patient, and—finally—respite is effected by intermittent or mild sedation and not continuous. Morita et al., *Terminal Sedation for Existential Distress*, 17 AM. J. HOSPICE & PALLIATIVE CARE 189, n's 4, 6–8 (2000).
See Quill and Byock, *supra* note 73 at 411, Table 1, Guidelines for Terminal Sedation and Voluntary Cessation of Eating and Drinking.
See also Thaddeus M. Pope and Lindsey E. Anderson, *Voluntarily Stopping Eating and Drinking: A Legal Treatment Option at The End of Life*, 17 WIDENER L. REV. 363 (2011); A. Alpers and Bernard Lo, *The Supreme Court Addresses Physician-Assisted Suicide: Can Its Rulings Improve Palliative Care?*, 8 ARCH. FAM. MED. 200 (1999).

92   Krakauer et al., *supra* note 66.
In the U.S., prosecutions are rare for "legitimate" physician assistance of terminally ill patients. *See* Alan Meisel et al., *Prosecutor and End-of-Life Decisionmaking*, 159 ARCH. INTERN. MED. 1089 (1999); LOANE SKENE, LAW AND MEDICAL PRACTICE 340 *passim* (3rd ed. 2008).

93   Krakauer et al., *supra* note 66 at 56, 57.

94   MARK A. LEVINE, AMERICAN MEDICAL ASS'N REPORT OF THE COUNCIL ON ETHICAL AND JUDICIAL AFFAIRS (CEJA), SEDATION TO UNCONSCIOUSNESS IN END-OF-LIFE CARE, CEJA REPORT 5-A-08, at 6 (2008) [hereinafter CEJA REPORT].
A comparable study was completed by the European Association for Palliative Care and released in 2009 as a ten-point framework for the use of sedation in palliative care. *See* 23 PALLIATIVE MED. 581 at 584 *passim* (2009). As with the American Medical Association Report, these procedural guidelines have been criticized for lacking a clear statement of the symptoms necessary to use palliative sedation and the primary party empowered to determine the propriety of its use—the patient or health care provider. *See* Niklas Juth et al., *European Association of Palliative Care (EAPC) Framework for Palliative Ethical Discussion*, 9 BMC Palliative Care 20 (2010) at http://www.biomedcentral.com/1472–684x/9/20.

DOI: 10.1057/9781137377395

95   CEJA REPORT, *id.* at 6.

96   *Id.*

97   *Id.*

98   *Id.* at 6, 7.

99   *Id.* at 7.

100   *Id.* at 7.

101   *Id.* at 7.

102   *Id.* at 7.

103   *Id.* at 4.

104   *Id.* at 5.

105   *Id.* at 5.

106   Margaret P. Battin, *Terminal Sedation: Pulling the Sheet Over Our Eyes*, 38 HASTINGS CENTER REP. 27, 29 (2008).

107   CEJA REPORT, *supra* note 94 at 5.

108   *Id.*

109   *Id.*

110   Battin, *supra* note 106.

111   *See* Ch. 4 *infra.*

112   *Id.*

DOI: 10.1057/9781137377395

4

Reconstructing the Principle of Double Effect

Abstract: *This chapter re-evaluates the Principle of Double Effect as it often manifests itself in health care decisions (typically involving the withdrawal of nutrition and hydration to the seriously ill) and suggests a way to improve its application as a construct for humane decisionmaking. Rather than ascertaining, under the Principle, when conduct is ethical—with undue emphasis being placed on the intent of an actor to pursue a course of action to achieve a good end—my proposal evaluates treatment/ non-treatment decisions, for example, by using only a cost/ benefit analysis of the proposed action. The appropriateness of terminal sedation as medical therapy is determined by analyzing whether the sedation is proportionate to the severity of suffering being reduced.*

George P. Smith. *Palliative Care and End-of-Life Decisions.* New York: Palgrave Macmillan, 2013.
DOI: 10.1057/9781137377395.

The principle of double effect—sometimes also stated to be either a doctrine or rule—is grounded in Roman Catholic philosophy and moral theology.[1] It proposes to structure specific guidelines to aid in determining when, ethically, it is permissible to pursue a course of action to achieve a good end—notwithstanding the full understanding that negative or bad results will, as well, flow from the initiating conduct.[2] The coverage and application of the principle has, over time, been embraced by philosophers and ethicists as having a profound relevance to assessing complex cases of health care ethics either in its classical application or by implication.[3] Indeed, it is contended that the principle has "improved care of the dying, and forms a common ground for competing notions of good care for the dying."[4]

For the conduct of the actor to be acknowledged as ethically permissible, four conditions must be met: the nature of the action must be good or morally neutral and, thus, not prohibited; a good effect or consequences must be intended to flow from the action, and not a bad or evil consequence; the good or positive result must not be used as a direct casual consequence of the evil result and the good or positive result must be proportionate to any evil result.[5] When all four conditions are met, the personal conduct of the agent being evaluated is held to be ethically permissible—this, even though an undesirable or "bad" result occurs.[6]

Moral distinctions or subtleties

In palliative care management, a moral distinction has all too often been recognized by some as an act between withdrawing treatment and withholding treatment—an omission.[7] And, accordingly, because of this ambiguous view point, it is asserted that a greater degree of accountability or responsibility must be assumed—legally—for the consequences of an individual's actions rather than his omissions.[8]

Subtle complexities infuse this taxonomical "distinction" because in the event a decision which leads to either an act or an omission is made, it does not necessarily, *ipso facto*, mean that its efficacy is grounded on a moral justification.[9] Rather, any such justification for treatment should be based primarily "on whether the care given or not given is appropriate to the patient's wishes [and] physical condition. ..." together with "certainty of [medical] progress."[10] Yet, the fact remains in palliative management,

DOI: 10.1057/9781137377395

society imposes moral and legal responsibility on care givers for both omissions as well as actions.[11]

In cases of artificial hydration—when a moral distinction is drawn between the withholding of treatment and the withdrawal of it[12]—greater blame may be given to the act of withdrawing treatment than withholding it.[13] When cases of this type are present, physicians become reluctant—if not unwilling—to commence treatment, even though medically appropriate, in order to avoid stopping it when it becomes subsequently inappropriate. The effect of this action may well result in undertreating at-risk patients.[14]

Another defensive response by physicians to the effort to chart a moral distinction between the withholding and withdrawal of treatment—which makes this putative moral distinction, itself, neither logical nor helpful—is seen in physician conduct which manifests itself in an unwillingness "to stop life-prolonging treatment when it is no longer appropriate because this constitutes a withdrawal of treatment—which is seen as potentially blameworthy, particularly, since it may contribute to the patient's death."[15] The end result when physician conduct of this nature occurs is that over-treatment may be the norm.[16]

Competing clinical intentions

Inasmuch as the doctrine of double effect analyzes two consequences flowing from an action and seeks to place a "substantive moral judgment" on the content of the intention of one action (and its consequences) as opposed to the other action,[17] the doctrine presents itself as a muddled template bereft of objective certainty for decisionmaking.[18]

Utilizing this doctrine in British and American courts requires a particularly astute pool of jurors who can ascertain whether a physician's intent was to either relieve suffering or cause death in the administration of pain relief. For the doctrine to be an efficacious tool for judicial decisionmaking, a physician is required to admit he administered lethal treatment with the primary intent to cause death. Given the criminal consequences of such a forthright admission, it would be unusual for a doctor to admit such a course of conduct.[19] Indeed, it would be common for a physician to have more than one intention, an awareness, or consideration that death will most likely occur from actions undertaken primarily to manage intractable pain.[20] Because of this duality of

DOI: 10.1057/9781137377395

competing or cross intents and the complexity of distinguishing between them, the requirement under the principle of double effect that a positive consequence be intended is exceedingly problematic. While legal terms such as intention and foresight appear to be neutral in a moral sense, in point of fact, they "relate to inherently moral issues" and perforce dictate ill-advised subjective moral judgments.[21]

The medical community asserts that the use of sedatives is not intended to hasten death.[22] Even though it is foreseen—as in cases of end-stage illness—that death will most certainly occur sooner than later with the use of terminal sedation, the fact that physicians maintain the practice is medically justifiable should be taken as conclusive.[23] And, were this proposition to be accepted, then, no valid need to question the application of the principle of double effect could be allowed. Yet, the fact remains, this "assurance" or "conclusion" is not accepted at face value as an honest professional judgment.[24] Even within the ranks of the medical profession, itself, although the principle is supported by most physicians and nurses, other care givers see it as but a "fig leaf" for euthanasia.[25] Rather, these individuals, together with some patients and their families, are blind-sided by the myth (quite often spread by the media) that analgesics (e.g., barbiturates more directly than opioids) are "nothing more than a polite way to kill the patient."[26]

Justifying double effect for palliative sedation

The central element for a justification of palliative sedation under the principle of double effect is to be found in the moral distinction drawn between the intentions of an actor, or physician, and the unintended—yet foreseen—consequences of the primary action. Taking the life of another is always, thus, morally impermissible; yet such actions which are foreseeable, but unintentional, may be permissible when the action produces proportionate good.[27] Put in context, then, even when a foreseen risk of hastened death is accepted, a physician may nonetheless order high doses of opioids and sedative in order to relieve patient suffering.[28] For ethicists, there is simply no clear line between efforts to relieve refractory systems and hastening death.[29] The *manner* by which a physician declares his intention, thus, is more determinative than what actions he takes under this doctrine. Ambiguity arises when physicians have, in various studies, admitted to double intentions when they administered

DOI: 10.1057/9781137377395

large doses of opioids: intentions to both decrease suffering and hasten death.[30]

Physician intent is irrelevant when the validity of a withdrawal of nutrition and hydration is raised; for, the operative issue is whether an individual patient is within his "liberty interest" in making this decision.[31]

> Regardless of whether clinical reality supports the concept of total patient autonomy on this issue, the legal precedent places this decision ultimately with the patient.... Legally, a physician's intent is irrelevant with respect to a patient's refusal or request for the withdrawal of a life-sustaining medical intervention. A physician's intent becomes a legal factor only when the physician takes an active, interventionist measure that could cause a patient's death.[32]

In contemporary society, legal liability is imposed upon those who foresee or should have foreseen the consequences of their actions which cause injury to another.[33] This legal standard is, accordingly, broadened considerably from one which, under the principle of double effect, limits the liability for only unintended consequences and, thus, may well characterize the principle as inconsistent with the standards of modern jurisprudence. The additional assumption made under the principle that it is morally wrong to cause or to hasten a moribund or terminally ill patient's death may also be rejected by those who disagree with this and become a reason for them to disregard the application of the principle altogether.[34]

Given these inherent weaknesses of the principle of double effect, it would be more efficacious to reformulate the justification for palliative sedation by examining proportionality rather than affirming intention. Accordingly, under proportionality, compassion and patient preferences are determinative. Rather than deal with oftentimes conflicting ethical guidelines to relieve patient suffering and yet not act in a way which causes death as a consequence, proportionality allows for a balancing of the guidelines. Thus if—for example—a physician believes it to be more compassionate to relieve refractory symptoms than to prolong life filled with physical torment for but a few hours, days, or a "few months," then—guided, as well, by patient preferences for sedative amount—palliative sedation may be administered properly within the bounds of good medical practice.[35] Sadly, there is a mistaken perception that death is always hastened by the aggressive administration of pain management.[36]

DOI: 10.1057/9781137377395

British courts have, over time, allowed palliative measures to be taken even though their incidental effect is to shorten life. The justification is to be found in a moral metaphor which acknowledges that physicians may limit suffering even though they may not put an immediate end to a patient's life. This metaphor of helping, rather than killing, may prove to be an invaluable psychological construct for the physician as well as an enlightened one for the courts. Under it, while a physician may know fully the consequences of his actions of increasing dosages of diamorphine for a patient, he need not describe the act nor be required by society to view it as "an act of killing."[37]

Rather than re-evaluate and test anew the principle of double effect by accepting this metaphor which is tied inextricably to the principle of compassion or mercy, the nuanced complexities of double effect are, essentially, subsumed under this metaphor. This re-statement—together with major emphasis on proportionality, which in turn brings in the mandate to avoid suffering—would go far to present a new contemporary construct for decisionmaking not mired in the quicksands of the "traditional" approach to testing with the principle of double effect applies.

Dosage and titration

If analgesics (e.g., barbiturates, opioids) are titrated to effect patient comfort, without intending to hasten patient death, this action—in and of itself—is perhaps the most valid indicator of a physician's intent and of particular importance in "validating" actions under the doctrine of double effect.[38] One of the rather predictable side effects of using opiates for pain relief is that sedation occurs.[39] Non-sedating agents are, of course, preferred but not always effective.[40]

In administering sedation for refractory pain, the goal of symptom relief should be sought initially by administering the lowest dosage[41]—one which neither suppresses respiration nor leads to respiratory distress.[42] Dosage which provides for no possibility for symptom relief *without* patient death could be termed properly as active euthanasia.[43] When lower dosages are ineffective, increased dosages are permissible.[44] But, there should be clear criteria, or clinical indications, to justify increased levels of medication and this—in turn—should be documented in the patient records and/or chart.[45]

Direct medical actions of this nature most usually occur when acute palliative care is made urgent because of sudden or severe patient

DOI: 10.1057/9781137377395

distress[46] owing to pain or other physical symptoms as well as psychological distress in the form of severe anxiety or agitated delirium.[47] As observed, the administration of the necessary medications (e.g., barbiturates, opioids and benzodiazepines), in order to give effective comfort and relief, often are accompanied by significant side effects which must be anticipated and explained to a patient's family and then managed.

Challenging traditional applications

Those who reject the rigid classical application of the principle of double effect assert that it is neither efficacious nor necessary in palliative care. If released from the principle's *raison d' entre* to provide an absolute safeguard against the intentional shortening of life and, instead, a position is that which recognizes that the benefits of relieving medical distress in cases of terminal illness may sometime outweigh the harm of shortening life through use of respite or terminal sedation, the principle becomes superfluous to palliative management.[48] Indeed, adoption of such a contemporary and humane policy would eliminate altogether the complex and finely nuanced arguments which seek to draw distinctions—sometimes hair splitting—between intending and foreseeing the effects of one's actions.[49] Re-structured as such, the principle of double effect would become a common sense approach to medico-legal-ethical decisionmaking and would—accordingly—appear to be in "accordance with the moral intuitions of most people."[50] Moreover, by re-formulating this template for decisionmaking and elevating compassion and proportionality to controlling values instead of merely seeking to prolong a life of suffering for those with end-stage illness by playing "shell games" of uncertainty and chance in determining the intentions of health care providers who are managing health care for those with terminal illness, a bold re-affirmation of beneficence, charity, compassion and mercy would be the controlling policies for action.[51]

The defense of necessity

In 1958, Glanville Williams put forward the proposition that in cases where a pain is so severe that its alleviation can no longer be achieved other than by administration of a lethal dosage of drugs, a medical

DOI: 10.1057/9781137377395

excuse should be recognized in law.[52] This excuse, then, would rest "upon the doctrine of necessity, there being at this juncture no way of relieving pain without ending life."[53] Accordingly, under a contemporary gloss for this suggestion, a physician could assert this defense to a charge of euthanasia or murder by showing that, by evaluating all circumstances surrounding[54] a patient's condition (and not focusing exclusively on a physician's intent), he acted in an effort to alleviate the severe or unbearable suffering of a patient.[55] And, furthermore, that his actions were taken in good faith and with a reasonable belief that they were a proportionate response to the patient's medical condition.[56] Factored into the validity of this legal defense would be another highly relevant factor: the extent to which, and frequency of, a competent patient's request for assistance in dying.[57] In a very real way, recognizing the defense of necessity is grounded in compassion.

Judicial guideposts

It is a given that moral questions are not settled by laws or legal arguments. And, it is truism that "all that is legal is not moral, and all that is moral is not necessarily legal."[58] Consequently, the extent to which legal arguments over the definition and use of assisted suicide or euthanasia have weighted morally is tied extricably to the extent to which they are "morally persuasive."[59] In this area of debate, it has been concluded that legal argumentation is faulty because it fails to address the moral complexities inherent in any discussion of hastened death.[60]

When the United States Supreme Court had an opportunity to advance a moral argument for accepting the rule of double effect in 1997 in *Vacco v. Quill*[61] and *Washington v. Glucksberg*[62]—although it invoked double effect reasoning—no moral arguments for accepting the rule or principle of double effect were proffered by the Court.[63] It has been suggested, however, that what the court did here was to lay a foundation for recognizing a constitutional right to adequate pain relief from dying.[64] And, within such a "right" to avoid suffering in dying, and to receive care, is—it is argued here—the co-ordinate right to receive terminal sedation when deemed reasonable by either a competent patient or a properly designated surrogate decision-maker. In cases of incompetency, this right would be exercised by an attending health care provider who determines this course of conduct is humane and compassionate and in the best interests of the patient. Action of this nature would be consistent with a physician's responsibility—and, indeed—commitment, to embrace the "ethics of compassionate response."[65]

Withdrawal of nutrition and hydration

That artificial nutrition and hydration are properly viewed as medical treatment and may, as such, be withdrawn if their continuation is evaluated as inconsistent with safeguarding the best interests of a patient, is legally sound and a medically valid position.[66] This rule was formulated as is seen as a right of refusal grounded in Due Process clause protections by the U.S. Supreme Court in 1997 in *Washington v. Glucksberg*.[67] Previously, in the 1990 case of *Cruzan v. Dir., Missouri Dept. of Health*, writing for the majority, Chief Justice Rhenquist "assumed" that there is a right, of a competent person, to refuse nutrition and hydration.[68] As such, this right of refusal is "inferred" from a constitutionally protected liberty interest—grounded in the doctrine of informed consent—for one to exercise their consent to refuse treatment.[69]

It remained for the Court, again, in 1997 to sharpen a necessary distinction between the withdrawal of life-sustaining treatment and physician-assisted suicide.[70] Crucial to this distinction is an understanding that while a patient who ingests a lethal dose of medication will, accordingly, be killed by such action, an underlying disease pathology will be the cause of death when one refuses life-sustaining treatment (e.g., nutrition and hydration).[71]

Going further in its effort to draw a clear distinction between the withdrawal of life-sustaining treatment considered by a patient to be "futile or degrading"[72] and physician-assisted suicide where the intention of the physician is to assure "that the patient be made dead,"[73] the court placed heavy emphasis upon the importance of intent as determinative and in doing so gave tacit approval for the use of terminal sedation. Very decisively, the court concluded that when evaluating the propriety of "induc[ing] barbiturate coma and then star[ving] [a patient] to death," palliative care may be administered which includes a decision to refuse the continuation of life-sustaining treatment—which may in turn "have the foreseen but unintended 'double effect' of hastening the patient's death."[74]

DOI: 10.1057/9781137377395

Justice Sandra Day O'Connor, writing a strong and eloquent concurring opinion in both *Glucksberg* and *Quill* endorsing the use of terminal sedation in palliative care,[75] concluded that while the Constitution did not grant any generalized right to "commit suicide," there was, however, a liberty interest in securing for mentally competent persons, experiencing great suffering, to control the manner in which their deaths occurred.[76]

Evaluating *Cruzan*, *Quill* and *Glucksberg* as a unit, and being mindful that the issue of the legality of terminal sedation as a final strategy for dealing with refractory pain was not directly before the Court, the use of terminal sedation as an integral part of palliative care and management was—nonetheless—endorsed, implicitly, by the Court.[77]

Clarifying standards for sedation, alimentation and hydration

In 2006, the American Academy of Hospice and Palliative Medicine issued a new position statement on artificial nutrition and hydration (ANH) in end-of-life care replacing, as such, its earlier statement on this issue in 2001.[78] Recognizing that artificial nutrition and hydration were developed originally to accommodate patients acutely ill and thus provide short-term care, the Academy also acknowledged current data which suggests these procedures neither prolong life nor prevent suffering.[79] Since patients in end-stage illnesses often lose both capacities to eat and drink, the ethical issue thus becomes whether—with no prospects for rehabilitation or recovery—nutrition or alimentation and hydration should be provided either upon request by patients, families, or care givers or, contrariwise, be withheld.

The Academy concluded that ANH should always be recognized as medical therapy and, as such, should be evaluated by balancing its costs and benefits (or benefits and burdens) "in light of the patient's goals of care and clinical circumstances."[80] While acknowledging that ANH has symbolic value and importance for some patients and their families, the Academy's position is that lines of communication be maintained among health care providers which deal not only in fears of starvation by afflicted patients and their families, but with clarifications of the clinical conditions which come with end-stage illness.[81] More specifically, patient information should be provided which explains that an individual's inability to both eat and drink are but part of the

DOI: 10.1057/9781137377395

"normal" process of dying.[82] Accordingly, when efforts at ANH are not advancing a patient's goals nor seen as consistent with sound clinical standards of practice[83]—and thus futile—they "can be ethically withheld or withdrawn."[84]

While there are reports that the use of terminal sedation is now endorsed by many hospices—with some even inducing coma with an added morphine drip to address unremitting pain[85]—the AAHPM's Statement on Palliative Sedation, issued in 2006 and, thus, different from its earlier position in 2001, is clear that palliative sedation be "proportionate to the patient's level of distress."[86] Reserved only for those cases with the "most severe, intractable suffering at the very end of life,"[87] palliative sedation to a level of unconsciousness is supported ethically and legally when three conditions are met: 1) The intent of the clinician is to relieve a patient's suffering; 2) The degree of sedation administered is proportionate to the severity of suffering being induced; and 3) Either an informed patient consent is obtained directly from the patient or his surrogate decision-maker—all consistent, as such, with the patient's treatment goals and personal values.[88]

This bold and compassionate action by the Academy is designed to educate the public to the validity of—under certain end-stage medically futile conditions—accepting physician-assisted death by integrating palliative care and its undergirding philosophies into a standard of appropriate care for the terminally ill.[89] By changing the taxonomical tone of analysis from the more traditional Physician-assisted Suicide (PAS) to Physician-assisted Death (PAD), the Academy is attempting to recast the very essence of the debate over the legality of receiving medical assistance in the dying process.[90]

Notes

1   Timothy E. Quill, Rebecca Dresser and Dan W. Brock, *The Rule of Double Effect—A Critique of Its Role in End-of-Life Decision Making*, 337 NEW ENG. J. MED. 1768 (1997).

2   *Id.*

3   RANDALL and DOWNIE, *supra* Ch. 1, note 17 at 73.

4   BARRY R. FURROW, et al., BIOETHICS: HEALTH CARE LAW AND ETHICS 10 (6th ed. 2008).

5   Quill et al., *supra* note 1.

6   *Id.*

DOI: 10.1057/9781137377395

Standing alone, without being tethered to the second condition, the undergirding policy supporting the principle of double effect is to be seen as validating ethically the use of medication in controlling pain—even when death may result. PELLEGRINO and THOMASMA, *supra* Ch. 1, note 70 at 176.

The Doctrine of Double Effect is ordinarily presumed to apply *only* to doctors because it is presumed that only doctors administer the medication to their patients. Since at the end-stage of life more and more medical care and decisionmaking is delegated to palliative care specialists and allied health professionals, it is arguable that these individuals should be able to assert a defense of necessity. Accordingly, they could assert that the administration of lethal pain medications had been delegated legally to them and that their use was compatible with maintaining the best interests of dying patients to be free of unremitting and existential pain. KERRIDGE, et al., *supra* Ch. 2, note 70 at 653.

7   RANDALL and DOWNIE, *supra* note 3 at 74.
     See also SMITH, *supra* Ch. 3, note 40 at 111–19.

8   RANDALL and DOWNIE, *supra* note 3.

9   *Id.*

10 *Id.*
     See generally James L. Bernat, *Chronic Disorders of Consciousness*, 367 THE LANCET 1181 (April 8, 2006); Laine C. Davidoff, *Patient-Centered Medicine: A Professional Evolution*, 275 JAMA 152 (1996).

11 RANDALL and DOWNIE *supra* note 3 at 74.

12 *Id.*

13 *Id.*
     See Daniel Callahan, *Terminal Sedation and The Artefactual Fallacy*, in TERMINAL SEDATION: EUTHANASIA IN DISGUISE at Ch. 9 (Torbjorn Tannsjo ed. 2004) (where it is concluded that actions which withdraw nutrition and hydration are morally legitimate).

14 RANDALL and DOWNIE *supra* note 3 at 74.

15 *Id.*

16 *Id.*

17 Suzanne Ost, *Euthanasia and The Defense of Necessity: Advocating a More Appropriate Legal Response* in THE CRIMINAL JUSTICE SYSTEM AND HEALTH CARE LAW at 103. (Charles A. Erin and Suzanne Ost eds. 2007).

18 *Id.* at 103, 104.

19 *Id.* at 105.

20 Bernard Lo and Gordon Rubenfeld, *Palliative Sedation in Dying Patients: "We Turn to It When Everything Else Hasn't Worked,"* 294 JAMA 1810, 1813 (2005).

21 Ost, *supra* note 17 at 103.

DOI: 10.1057/9781137377395

See Lo and Rubenfeld, *supra* note 20 at 1810 (questioning whether dosage size is determinative of intent); Timothy E. Quill, *The Ambiguity of Clinical Intentions* 329 N. ENG. J. MED. 1039 (1993) (suggesting proportionality of treatments is crucial to discerning clinical intent); Williams, *supra* Ch. 2, note 27 at 41, 46.

22 Williams *id.* at 46.

23 *Id.*

24 *Id.*

25 *Id.*

26 *Id.*

27 *See* Timothy E. Quill et al., *Palliative Options of Last Resort: A Comparison of Voluntarily Stopping Eating and Drinking, Terminal Sedation, Physician-Assisted Suicide, and Voluntary Active Euthanasia,* 278 JAMA 2099, 2101 *passim* (1947). *See also* SHAI J. LAVI, THE MODERN ART OF DYING 129–34 (2005); GEORGE P. SMITH, II, FINAL CHOICES: AUTONOMY IN HEALTH CARE DECISIONS 101–09 (1989).

28 Lo and Rubenfeld *supra* note 20 at 1812.

29 *Id.* at 1813.
   See 1 ALAN MEISEL, THE RIGHT TO DIE § 8.2 at 470 (2nd ed. 1995).

30 *Id.*
   See LAVI, *supra* note 27.

31 McStay, *supra* Ch. 2, note 33 at 45, 60.

32 *Id.*

33 DAN B. DOBBS, THE LAW OF TORTS 334 (2000).
   See PROSSER AND KEETON ON THE LAW OF TORTS at 169, 290, 303 (W. Page Keeton, Dan B. Dobbs, Robert E. Keeton and David G. Owen eds., 5th ed. 1984).

34 Lo and Rubenfeld *supra* note 20 at 1813.

35 *Id.*
   See Joseph Boyle, *Enriching Proportionalism Through Christian Narrative in Bioethics: The Decisive Development in Richard McCormick's Moral Theory?,* 24 CHRISTIAN BIOETHICS 302, 304, 306–08 (2008) (analyzing proportionalism as a method "for justifying moral norms and judgments in the light of basic goods").

36 FURROW et al., *supra* note 4.

37 Alexander McCall Smith, *Euthanasia: The Strengths of The Middle Ground,* 7 MEDICAL L. REV. 195, 206–07 (1999).

38 Krakauer et al., *supra* Ch. 3, note 66.

39 *Id.*

40 *Id.*

41 *Id.*

42 Lo and Gordon Rubenfeld, *supra* note 20 at 1812.

DOI: 10.1057/9781137377395

43   *Id.*
     See LAVI, *supra* note 27.

44   *Id.*
     For the conscious patient, reports of continued pain, displays of agitation, restlessness and confusion and/or respiratory distress or myoclonus, would be grounds for dosage increases. For the unconscious patient, unable to report levels of distress, it remains for health care providers to access levels of discomfort (e.g., furrowed brow, tachypnea and other symptomatologies associated with suffering). *Id.* 1811, 1813.

45   Lo and Rubenfeld *supra* note 20 at 1813.
     Efforts of the American Medical Association Council on Ethical and Judicial Affairs to "clarify" the medically proper uses for palliative sedation, and specifically dosage distinctions have been termed "naive in the extreme." Margaret P. Battin, *Terminal Sedation: Pulling the Sheet Over Our Eyes*, 38 HASTINGS CENTER RPT. 27, 29 (2008). The Council's effort to infer physician intent from the pattern of practice in dosage states, "one large dose" or "rapidly accelerated doses of morphine may signify a bad intention (seeking to cause death) while "repeated doses or continuous infusions are benign. Report of The Council on Ethical and Judicial Affairs, *Sedation to Unconsciousness in End-of-Life Care*, CEJA Report 5-A-08 at 5 (2008). Battin argues convincingly that "repeated dosage and continuous infusions" could well be taken as "a clever attempt to cover one's tracks." Battin, *id.* at 29.

46   Krakauer et al., *supra* note 38 at 60.

47   *Id.*

48   RANDALL and DOWNIE, *supra* note 3 at 73.

49   *Id.*

50   *Id.*
     See Boyle, *supra* note 35 at 307 (discussing how, under proportionalism, not only are moral absolute rejected, but also the traditional doctrine of double effect).

51   *See* Timothy E. Quill, *The Ambiguity of Clinical Institutions* 329 N. ENG. J. MED. 1039 (1993) (arguing that proportionality should be the central focus for evaluating decisions of this nature).

52   GLANVILLE WILLIAMS, THE SANCTITY OF LIFE IN THE CRIMINAL LAW 286–88 (1958).
     If there is "no way of relieving pain without ending life," the defense of necessity should be allowed. WILLIAMS, *id.* Yet, when other pain management therapies are available and effective, this defense would not be available to physicians nor would it be allowed when evidence established lethal drugs were administered which had "no analgesic or sedative effect." KERRIDGE, et al., *supra* Ch. 2, note 70 at 652. The defense of necessity has been available as a valid defense to murder in the U.K. since 2000. *Id.,* citing

Re A [2000] 4 All ER 961 at 1051 (Brooke LJ); R v Latimer [2001] 193 DLR (4th) 577 at 596.

53 *Id.* at 288.

54 Ost, *supra* note 17 at 115–16.

55 *Id.*
"A common sense notion of medical duty" to respond in end-stage care is not only established but validated, clinically, from either quantitative or qualitative evaluations of medical futility. Lawrence J. Schneiderman et al., *Medical Futility: Its Meaning and Ethical Implications,* in BIOETHICS: AN INTRODUCTION TO THE HISTORY, METHODS, AND PRACTICE 409 (Nancy S. Jecker et al., eds., 2nd ed. 2007).

56 Ost, *supra* note 17 at 115–16; British Crown Prosecution Service Guidelines, *supra* Ch. 2 at note 68.

57 Ost, *supra* note 17 at 116.
The three elements of the defense of necessity could be established by utilizing the reasoning of the doctrine of double effect. Accordingly, when it could be established that a physician's action were undertaken in response to a patient's intractable pain (and not to accelerate death) for which there was no reasonable alternative course of treatment and that this action was in turn "proportionate to the risk of a lengthy and painful dying process," the defense should be allowed. KERRIDGE, et al., *supra* Ch. 2, note 70 at 652.

58 Daniel P. Sulmasy and Edmund D. Pellegrino, *The Rule of Double Effect: Clearing Up The Double Talk,* 159 ANNALS INTERNAL MED. 545 (1999).

59 *Id.* at 548.

60 *Id.*
But see Edward Rabin, *Assisted Suicide, Morality, and Law: Why Prohibiting Assisted Suicide Violates The Establishment Clause,* 63 VAND. L. REV. 763, 773–78, 791, 797, 810–11 (2010) (asserting that since existing laws prohibiting assisted suicide have derived—historically—from a Christian morality of higher purpose and, thus, favor and indeed coerce a particular religious morality, these laws are violative of the Establishment Clause of the Constitution; instead, laws should reflect a standard of self-fulfillment which in turn would allow pursuit of values for a satisfying life which do not harm others).

61 117 S. CT. 2293 (1997).

62 *Id.* at 2258.

63 Sulmasy and Pellegrino, *supra* note 58 at 548.
But see Marc Spindelman, *Death, Dying and Domination,* 106 MICH. L. REV. 1641 at 1661, n. 60 (concluding that Glucksberg constitutionalized the principle of double effect).

64 Robert A. Burt, *The Supreme Court Speaks—Not Assisted Suicide but a Constitutional Right to Palliative Care,* 337 NEW ENG. J. MED. 1234 (1997).

DOI: 10.1057/9781137377395

65   ALBERT R. JONSEN, THE NEW MEDICINE AND THE OLD ETHIC 49 (1990).
     In cases of incompetency, the physician has a special fiduciary-type "obligation to act as a steward of the patient's moral right to have his or her wishes fulfilled." While not a type of moral warrant for a physician to impose a personal set of values or make the advancement of a medical good the controlling principle, neither does this act of "beneficence-in-trust" mean that a physician submit "slavishly and uncritically to decisions made by a surrogate." Instead, "the obligation of that stewardship is to clarify, validate and enhance the patient's will to the extent possible." PELLEGRINO and THOMASMA, *supra* note 6 at 162.
     See Alexander A. Kon, *The Shared Decision-Making Continuum*, 304 JAMA 903 (Aug. 25, 2010).

66   Washington v. Glucksberg, 521 U.S. 702 at 736–37 (O'Connor, J. concurring). *See generally* Lois L. Shepherd, *Dignity and Autonomy after Washington v. Glucksberg, An Essay About Abortion Death and Dignity*, 7 CORNELL J. L. and PUB. POL'Y 431 (1998).

67   Washington v. Glucksberg, 521 U.S. at 720–23.

68   497 U.S. 261, 279 (1990).

69   *Id.* at 270.
     See David Casarett et al., *Appropriate Use of Artificial Nutrition and Hydration—Fundamental Principles and Recommendations*, 353 NEW ENG. J. MED. 2607 (Dec. 15, 2005).

70   Vacco v. Quill, 521 U.S. 793, 801 (1997) (Stevens, J.).

71   *Id.*

72   Smith, *supra* Ch. 2, note 47.

73   Vacco v. Quill, 521 U.S. 793 at 801–02.

74   *Id.* at 807, n. 11.

75   She was joined by Justice Ginsberg and, in part, by Justice Breyer. Washington v. Glucksberg at 521 U.S. 702 at 736–37.

76   Washington v. Glucksberg, 521 U.S. 702 at 736.

77   McStay, *supra* note 31 at 53.
     On August 1, 2007, The Congregation for The Doctrine of Faith published, with approval, *Responses to Certain Questions of The U.S. Conference of Catholic Bishops* which acknowledges, in principle, that nutrition and hydration are both "an ordinary and proportionate means of preserving life" and "therefore obligatory." Similarly, for patients in a permanent vegetative state, who are being maintained artificially with nutrition and hydration, there can be no discontinuance of this care even when a medical judgment is made that patient consciousness will never occur. FURROW et al., *supra* note 4 at 310–11.
     The authority and force of this means of policymaking has been questioned when other more established vehicles for setting policy in this

are available. *Id.* at 311 referencing John Hardt and Kevin O'Rourke, *Nutrition and Hydration: The Congregation for the Doctrine of Faith*, In Perspective, 88 HEALTH PROGRESS 1 (2007). FURROW et al., *id.* at 310–11.

But see U.S. Bishops' Pro-Life Committee, *Nutrition and Hydration: Moral and Pastoral Reflections* in BIOETHICS: AN INTRODUCTION TO THE HISTORY METHODS AND PRACTICE, at 417, 419, (Nancy S. Jecker et al., eds. 2nd ed. 2007) where, under Moral Principles (5), the Committee concluded in 1996: "In the final stage of dying one is not obliged to prolong the life of a patient by every possible means: 'When inevitable death is imminent in spite of the means used, it is permitted in conscience to take the decision to refuse forms of treatment that would only secure a precarious and burdensome prolongation of life, so long as the normal care due to the sick person in similar cases is not interrupted.' "

See also ARTIFICIAL NUTRITION AND HYDRATION AND THE PERMANENTLY UNCONSCIOUS PATIENT: THE CATHOLIC DEBATE (Ronald P. Hamel and James J. Walter eds. 2007); Alan Sanders, *The Clinical Reality of Artificial Nutrition and Hydration for Patients at The End of Life*, 9 NAT'L CATH. BIOETHICS Q. 293 (2009).

78 Position Statements, Statement on Artificial Nutrition and Hydration Near the End of Life, American Academy of Hospice and Palliative Medicine, approved December 8, 2006, http://www.aahpsm.org/positions/nutrition.html, (accessed October 14, 2007).

See generally H. R. Pasman et al., *Forgoing Artificial Nutrition and Hydration in Nursing Home Patients with Dementia*, 19 ALZHEIMER DIS. ASSOC. DISORDER J. 154 (July–Sept. 2004); Alan Meisel, *Barriers to Forgoing Nutrition and Hydration in Nursing Homes*, 21 AM. J. L. and MED. 335 (1995).

79 *Id.*

See DANIEL CALLAHAN, THE TROUBLED DREAM OF LIFE, 80–2 (2000) (observing that artificial nutrition and hydration were originally for short-term treatments for post surgical patients but, over the years, have been transformed into Basic Care rather than regarded as treatment—this, in spite of the fact that the process of dying is recognized as being accompanied by the inability to take food and water).

Survival rates for patients with advanced dementia do not appear to increase when artificial nutrition and hydration are given. LOIS L. SHEPHERD, IF THAT EVER HAPPENED TO ME: MAKING LIFE DECISIONS AFTER SCHIAVO 155 (2009).

80 Position Statement, *supra* note 78.

81 *Id.*

82 *Id.*

Some states have drawn very artificial and illogical distinctions between withholding and withdrawing artificial nutrition (which may be refused)

DOI: 10.1057/9781137377395

and hand and spoon feeding (which may not). SHEPHERD, *supra* note 79 at 148–52 (2009). In point of fact, there are currently no legal standards which justify such distinctions. *Id.* at 152.

See, e.g., 16 DEL. CODE § 2501 (c) (2008) where spoon or bottle feeding is not included within the definition of artificial nutrition and hydration and requires a precise written directive before it will be withheld. *See also* the Model Starvation and Dehydration of Persons with Disabilities Prevention Act, SHEPHERD, *id.* at 189–91.

83 Position Statement, *supra* note 78.

84 *Id.*
Charlotte F. Allen, *Back Off!, I'm Not Dead Yet!*, WASH. POST, Oct. 14, 2007, at B1.

85 *See generally* Balfour Mount, *Morphine Drips, Terminal Sedation, and Slow Euthanasia: Definitions and Facts, Not Anecdotes*, 12 J. PALLIATIVE CARE 31 (1996).

86 Position Statements, Statement on Palliative Sedation, American Academy of Hospice and Palliative Medicine, http://www.aahpm.org/positions/sedation. html (accessed 10/14/2007).

87 *Id.*

88 *Id.*

89 Position Statements, Physician-Assisted Death, American Academy of Hospice and Palliative Medicine, http://www.aahpm.org/positions/suicide. html (accessed October 14, 2008).
What is appropriate care under any given set of circumstances must be adjusted as medical conditions change. Thus, a duty to provide care should never be understood as a "perpetual obligation" to provide artificial nutrition and hydration. SHEPHERD, *supra* note 79 at 145.

90 *See* Smith, *supra* Ch. 2, note 34 (arguing for a taxonomical change in terminology which accepts use of enlightened self-determination or assisted rational suicide rather than assisted suicide).

DOI: 10.1057/9781137377395

5
Physician Assistance at Death or Euthanasia?

Abstract: *This chapter confronts the glaring ambiguities of definition and use in distinguishing physician assisted suicide from euthanasia. Taxonomies of confusion should yield to the clinical experience or praxis of humane and compassionate care at the conclusion of life. Wise policy dictates confusing ethical and religious directives and interpretations be secondary to a medical assessment of end-of-life care adjusted by a situation ethic shaped by beneficence and palliation. This approach is preferred to a rigid, unyielding* a priori *ethic which mandates care—rehabilitative or curative—when, in reality, such treatment is not licit.*

George P. Smith. *Palliative Care and End-of-Life Decisions.* New York: Palgrave Macmillan, 2013. DOI: 10.1057/9781137377395.

As a matter of principle, it is difficult to find and defend present distinctions between physician-assisted suicide and euthanasia.[1] Instead of falling into a taxonomical quagmire, it has been more traditional to assess—clinically—a patient's condition by determining whether the condition is curative, rehabilitative, or palliative.[2] The principle of medical futility, as seen, has been most helpful, if not determinative, in making a medical assessment; for, by its use and implementation, physicians have clear markers, if not protocols, for non-treatment.[3] Consistent with the failure to find an emerging national cognizance to a right or liberty interest to enlist assistance from a physician in ending life,[4] state courts—save one in Montana[5]—have neither found a right to physician-assisted suicide within their state constitutions nor have state legislatures, other than in Oregon[6] and Washington,[7] legalized this type of action[8] in the years following the Supreme Court's decision in *Washington* et al., v. *Glucksberg* et al.[9]

Interestingly, the Supreme Court of British Columbia—consistent with the progressive spirit of the Montana Supreme Court[10]—held in June 2012 that provisions in the Criminal Code of Canada prohibiting assisted death "unjustifiably infringe" the equality rights and the rights to life, liberty, and security guaranteed by the Canadian Charter of Rights and Freedoms.[11] In order for judicial appeals of this decision to take their course and for Parliament to consider and address this legislative weakness of the Code, a constitutional exemption from the Code's provision was granted to the moving party, Gloria Taylor. This exemption, then, has the practical effect of allowing Taylor, who suffers from a neurodegenerative disorder known as Lou Gehrig's disease, to arrange a physician-assisted death if she wishes. The Court held wisely that medical assistance at death can be sought by competent individuals terminally ill and near death with no hope of recovering, who are suffering from enduring and serious physical or psychological distress which is intolerable and cannot be alleviated by any medical or other treatment acceptable to the at-risk patient.[12] Before the appeal was perfected, Gloria died on October 8, 2012, of an infection caused by a perforated colon.[13]

Rather than continue efforts to find meaningful distinctions between suicide and assisted suicide, it is less confusing to structure a dialogue grounded in references to compassionate aid in dying or physician-assisted dying.[14] Indeed, since *Glucksberg*, the essence of assisted suicide is not really germane to any discussion of end-of-life care since the recognition of terminal or palliative sedation was validated there.[15]

DOI: 10.1057/9781137377395

The scope of personal autonomy

If personal autonomy, or "the right to define one's own concept of exist-ence" and "the mystery of human life,"[16] extends arguably to the very time and manner of one's death,[17] it has been asserted, logically, that this fundamental right should not be limited necessarily to the terminally ill[18] and the "seriously ill or impaired who are suffering or in pain."[19] Indeed, others have expressed concern that if this right is recognized nationally, it will most assuredly be asserted indiscriminately to the "seriously ill or impaired who are suffering in pain"[20] and not invoked on behalf of the terminally ill.[21]

Specifically, concerns have been raised that the standard of terminal ill-ness, in and of itself, is inadequate to measure certain medical conditions which exceed a diagnosis of life expectancy beyond, for example, the more "normal" period of three months[22] or six months.[23] Three specific scenarios have been posited as being dangerous because of the "open-ended" or limitless nature of present evaluations of terminal illness:[24] cases where patients might be suffering from Lou Gehrig's disease yet not diagnosed fully as suffering from the end-stage of the disease; or, where a patient, afflicted with paralysis from the neck down, can survive with palliative care for some 20 years; or, finally, where a patient is in the early stages of Alzheimer's disease.[25]

In each of these hypotheticals, no rigid time-line can be imposed on a patient's personal standard of hopelessness. If an informed unilateral decision is made to end one's life in the early stages of Alzheimer's dis-ease before levels of incompetence and indignity occurs, then—surely—that decision must be accepted. The principle of medical futility applies equally to all three scenarios because, put simply, there is neither curative care nor rehabilitation available. Rather than be concerned with the mis-application of the terminal illness standard in these three specific cases, the opportunity to embrace widely, with human compassion and mercy, individuals presenting with these sympathologies should be accepted as futile—this, simply because there is no hope for a qualitative recovery.[26]

The realities of the persistent vegetative state

The absence of rehabilitation or qualitative recovery is seen vividly—without question—in patients present in a persistent vegetative state

(PVS). Cases of this nature present a particularly vexatious medico-legal and ethical conundrum: namely, what type of care or "treatment" is appropriate for those who are unaware and insensate, unable to self-feed, have lost all language capabilities, yet can often breathe spontaneously, are capable of some degree of movement and not comatose?[27] A secondary issue is whether a diagnosis of PVS is properly considered to be a futile or terminal condition. Once a subsequent prognosis of no recovery has been made with a "very high level of certainty," should alimentation and hydration be recognized as proper medical treatment or "basic, required care?"[28]

Although analysis of the general issue of withdrawal of nutrition and hydration has been presented,[29] it has a special complexity when viewed within the context of PVS. Central to any evaluation of the medical consequences of one being in a PVS is an understanding of the difference between this condition and brain death—for, "in the former, the patient is 'awake' and can execute some motions, although lack consciousness [and, thus, cognitive neurological function] but in the latter, the patient is comatose."[30] With both conditions, there is neither rehabilitation nor recovery.[31] Once the capacity for consciousness is lost totally and irreversibly, one may be properly considered to be dead[32] and is often classified as suffering "higher brain death."[33] Interestingly, brain stem death is different from higher brain death. In the former, generally, the brain stem and the remainder of the brain is dead, but, only the cerebral cortices are dead in the latter.[34] In any of these four conditions, it is obvious that afflicted patients are incapable of achieving "relational capacity" with other individuals and—thus—should be given no treatment other than palliative care.[35]

The Terri Schiavo tragedy

The profoundly tragic case of Terri Schiavo is a dramatic paradigm of societal confusion and misunderstanding of the PVS condition and its fatal consequences.[36]Although not significantly different from other similar cases resolved on a weekly, if not daily basis, without resort to state and national legislative bodies and various levels of the judiciary,[37] Terri's ordeal became complicated and protracted because there was no consensus to be found either with Terri's family or her husband regarding what course of medical care was in her "best interests" and consistent

DOI: 10.1057/9781137377395

with her previous pre-disability health care wishes.[38] Viewed, alternatively, as not only a "failure of ethical decision-making by her family" and her husband as well as the courts,[39] but as a failed experiment of the American political system "in which rational decision-making was overwhelmed by vitriolic special interest groups,"[40] Terri's ordeal lasted some 15 years.[41]

Initially incapacitated on February 25, 1990 when—at age 26—she had a heart attack and lost consciousness, Terri's subsequent diagnosis of being in a PVS occurred on October 2002. She was maintained until March 18, 2005, when artificial nutrition and hydration were withdrawn by court order and she died March 31, 2005.[42] Inasmuch as Terri was consciously unaware that she was being fed—or even had been fed—a central argument could have been made that this care was not basic care.[43]

Religious concerns

A revised 2009 Directive for Catholic Health Care Services issued by the U.S. Conference of Catholic Bishops continues to be a source of debate regarding the extent to which there is a moral obligation to provide nutrition and hydration to patients who cannot take food orally and specifically those in a chronic and irreversible state (e.g., persistently vegetative).[44] Essentially, one school of analysis holds that this directive is consistent with traditional Catholic views for end-of-life care[45] and allows a person to forego or withdraw life-sustaining treatment in some circumstances where the burden of treatment outweigh the benefits it provides and it would be taken as futile.[46] Others assert the newly revised directive requires medically administered nutrition and hydration by "asserting that extension of unconscious life is always a benefit to the person" and—furthermore—"narrows the scope of morally relevant burdens of treatment to those burdens experienced by the patient alone."[47]

When there are, as here, striking differences of interpretative opinion regarding the application and scope of ethical and religious directives for end-of-life care, this can add a layer of confusion for courts and health care professionals as they grapple with determining the values and interests of a dying patient.[48] In cases where critically ill or dying patients have failed to execute advance health care directives, a family's religious beliefs may compel a particular treatment decision.[49] Often,

DOI: 10.1057/9781137377395

in right-to-die cases in opposition to an articulated state interest in the sanctity of life, religious beliefs may direct termination of treatment.[50] In medical futility, a family's "faith-based adherence to vitalist principles may clash with physicians' reliance on the statistical improbability that the treatment will benefit the patient."[51] For the law to be guided accurately and correctly by what is a patient's best interests with respect to the religious beliefs of the patient as advanced or interpreted by his family, these beliefs must be presented forthrightly and not be competitive.

While respecting the beliefs of patients and their families, it has been suggested that these beliefs, "raw intuitive judgments, abstract principles and theoretical frameworks" cohere logically.[52] Termed the Principle of Secular Rationality, this notion requires secular reasons for advocating or supporting either laws or public policies which restrict human conduct.[53]

Issues of rationality and religious beliefs come into direct focus when, for example, a family is unable to accept neurological criteria for certifying death. New York state hospitals have been grappling with this issue for a number of years. In 2001, hospital policies sought to accommodate family religions, moral or ethical objections, to a declaration of brain death up to a period of 24 hours.[54] If issues remained unresolved, hospital policy authorized cessation of treatment and support services (e.g., medications and artificial nutrition and hydration).[55] New York law—unlike that in New Jersey which apparently is the only state mandating insurance coverage during a period of accommodation—does not obligate health care following a determination of neurological death.[56] Ancillary to this issue of a certification of neurological death is the equally vexatious issue of the extent to which health care providers have an ethical and legal right to provide care which they consider unreasonable and medically futile.[57]

The limits of state interest

Foundational to the recognition of a "right" to privacy from governmental intrusions were the U.S. Supreme Court decisions in *Griswold v. Connecticut*[58] and *Eistenstadt v. Baird*.[59] These decisions became crucial to the Court's decision in *Lawrence v. Texas* in 2003 which held the Texas Homosexual Conduct Law was an unconstitutional abridgment of the right to liberty under the Due Process Clause.[60] Accordingly, the Court determined, sexual intimacy among same-sex couples was a freedom not limited by any spatial bounds.[61] Rather, the liberty of persons must be recognized inherently "an autonomy of self that includes freedom of thought, belief, expression, and certain intimate conduct."[62] People are entitled to "dignity as free persons."[63] It is posited that, over time, based on *Lawrence*, a fundamental right to physician-assisted suicide may be found in the Constitution.[64] For the "foreseeable future," however, the *Glucksberg* rule remains.[65]

There must be limits to the state's *parens patriae* powers to interfere with autonomous and informed decisions by citizens who wish to be relieved of their pain and suffering—which, as such, is the result of medical conditions which are properly evaluated as futile with no curative hope of rehabilitation or sustained qualitative existence, mentally, or physically. Indeed, "there is a realm of personal liberty which the government may not enter."[66] Linked with this right of self-determination is the equally important right to beneficent treatment which advances the best interests of the distressed patient as determined by the patient, himself.[67] These two rights are fundamental to any and all decisions regarding health care treatment.[68] When considering terminally ill patients or those diagnosed as having a futile medical condition, the state's general interest in protecting—and in some cases enforcing a continuance of life which has little if any quality—surely must be qualified or trumped by the right of self-determination to make one of life's most intimate, private decision, namely death.[69]

Resolving ambiguity: toward a resolution—state action

The idea, and what appears to be a growing practice, of addressing the issue of physician-assisted suicide or death by conjoining this practice with proper efforts to manage intractable pain may well prove to be the very construct for accepting, and later validating, medical assistance in hastening death in those cases where it is deemed medically proper and humane.[70] State statutes are being enacted which allow for the delivery of "adequate pain relief" and exempt this conduct from liability, both under criminal law and/or state medical licensing guidelines. So long as these medical actions are "in accord with accepted guidelines" for relieving intractable pain, they are deemed legitimate and lawful.[71] This approach to resolving ambiguity serves as a metric or construct for reasonable,

DOI: 10.1057/9781137377395

compassionate, and rational medical decisionmaking in cases of medical futility and end-of-life care.

The two fundamental—and, indeed, conflicting—beliefs which shape this whole area of death management and palliative care are forever in flux and incapable of complete resolution. As seen, one school of thought champions personal dignity, autonomy, and beneficence in cases of terminal illness.[72] Others seek to protect "all human life, no matter how poor the quality."[73] Choices, indubitably, "tragic choices,"[74] must be made in managing a good, compassionate death. These two philosophies of care are "accommodated," or assuaged, by a societal force that—while continuing to maintain a strong resistance to the legalization of physician-assisted suicide or active euthanasia—nonetheless allows the underground practice of both[75] and deemphasize the prosecution of this conduct.[76]

In the final analysis, end-of-life care should be assessed and adjusted on a case-by-case basis using the metric proposed herein—a metric always guided by a situational ethic anchored in beneficence and palliation rather than a rigid and unyielding *a priori* ethic of mandated rehabilitative or curative care.[77] Rather than be shackled to taxonomies of confusion in end-of-life care—such as euthanasia, suicide, physician-assisted suicide, and vitalism—the clinical experience or praxis of humane, common sense care at the conclusion of life should be determinative.

Notes

1   Yale Kamisar, *Foreword: Can Glucksberg Survive Lawrence? Another Look at The End of Life and Personal Autonomy*, 106 MICH. L. REV. 1453, 1474 (2008).
     See RICHARD A. POSNER, AGING AND OLD AGE 235–45 (1995) (maintaining that there should be a right to assisted suicide); Len Doyal, *Why Active and Physician-Assisted Suicide Should be Legalized*, 323 BR. MED. J. 1079 (2001).
     See also Charles H. Baron et al., *A Model State Act to Authorize and Regulate Physician Assisted Suicide*, 33 HARV. J. LEGISLATION 1, 10 (1996).
     Interestingly, in *Vacco*, the Supreme Court found no legal relevance between the classic distinctions between either active or passive euthanasia or, as well, between "the provision of artificial fluids and nutrition and other medical interventions." George J. Annas, *The Bell Tolls for a Constitutional Right to Physician-Assisted Suicide*, 337 NEW ENG. J. MED. 1098, 1102 (Oct. 9, 1997). What was, however, seen as determinative by the court was causation and

DOI: 10.1057/9781137377395

physician intent in prescribing or in administering medications which have a direct or even indirect role in hastening death. *Id.*

The New York State Task Force on Life and the Law, in issuing its 1997 supplemental report to its 1994 Report, *When Death is Sought*, concluded that valid distinctions between assisted suicide, the refusal of treatment, and the administration of high opioid dosages for refractory pain were essential for coherent policies in end-of-life medical care and that the latter two treatments should in no way be considered an act of euthanasia. Committee on Care at The End of Life, Institute of Medicine 12 (1997).

2   *See* Marc Sapir, *The Spectrum of Medical Care: Curative, Rehabilitative and Palliative*, 279 JAMA 20 (1998); Ellen Fox *Predominance of The Curative Model of Medical Care: A Residual Program*, 278 JAMA 761 (1997).
   See also R. Sean Morrison and Albert L. Siu, *Survival in End-Stage Dementia Following Acute Illness*, 284 JAMA 47 (July 5, 2000) (asserting that for patients with advanced dementia who have suffered hip fractures or pneumonia and have limited life expectancies, care designed to minimize pain and discomfort should be the preferred goal); Sachs, *supra* Ch. 1, note 7.

3   Smith, *supra* Ch. 2, note 47.

4   Kamisar, *supra* note 1 at 1467.

5   Although not declaring a constitutional right to die with dignity, the Montana Supreme Court held in December, 2009, that—under the state's Rights of The Terminally Ill Act—competent, terminally ill patients can request physicians assistance in obtaining a prescription for a lethal dose of medicine to be self-administered; and, further, the Act shields physicians from civil or criminal liability for any such assistance. Baxter v. Montana, DA-0051, 2009 MT. 449. *See* Kirk Johnson, *Ruling by Montana Supreme Court Bolsters Physician Assisted Suicide*, N.Y. TIMES, Jan. 1, 2010, at A17.

6   ORE. REV. STAT. §§127.800(12), 127.805 (2005).

7   REV. CODE WASH. ANN., Ch. 70, 245 (2009).
   See Ch. 1, *supra* at note 52 regarding the defeat in Massachusetts of similar legislation and the new Vermont statute on assisted dying.

8   Kamisar, *supra* note 1 at 1467.
   In reality, in the U.S., prosecutorial discretion is exercised commonly and seen in refusals by the state to prosecute cases of death assistance when the questioned conduct is within legal and professional boundaries—this, because there is simply wide acceptance of physician-assisted death. Meisel, *supra* Ch. 3, note 92; SKENE, *supra* Ch. 3 note 92.
   See supra Ch. 2, Skoloff, note 68 (reporting on a 2013 case in Arizona where the judicial process, in essence, acknowledged the alleviation of suffering as a valid consideration for a sentence for manslaughter).

9   521 U.S. 702 (1997).

10 Johnson, *supra* note 5.

DOI: 10.1057/9781137377395

11   Carter v. Canada (Attorney General), 2012 BCSC 886.
      The sections within the Charter found to be abridged were 7, 15, and 52.

12   *Id.*

13   Had Ms. Taylor not died, The Court of Appeals would have likely heard
      a full appeal of the new case in the Spring of 2013—with leave to appeal
      subsequently to the Supreme Court of Canada probably in 2014, with a
      distinct possibility that the Court would, in turn, overrule the 1993 decision
      in *Rodriguez v. British Columbia* (Attorney General), 3 S.C.R. 519 which held
      the prohibition on assisted suicide in the Criminal Code of Canada was not
      contrary to the Canadian Charter of Rights and Freedoms. James S. Keller,
      [Appeals] Court [Judge] upholds Gloria Taylor's right to die, THE CALGARY
      HERALD, Aug. 12, 2012, at 1. Interestingly, an appeal on the issue of the
      constitutionality of the Criminal Code's assisted suicide prohibition was
      nonetheless heard in March, 2013, by the British Columbia Court of Appeal
      and then, will ultimately go to the Supreme Court as anticipated.

14   Kathryn L. Tucker, *In the Laboratory of the States: The Progress of Glucksberg's
      Invitation to States to Address End-of-Life Choices*, 106 MICH. L. REV. 1593
      (2008).
      See TOM L. BEAUCHAMP, STANDING ON PRINCIPLE Ch. 7 (2010)
      (discussing when hastened death is neither killing nor letting die).
      See also CARLOS G. PRADO, CHOOSING TO DIE: ELECTIVE DEATH
      AND MULTICULTURISM Chs. 2, 3 (2008) (discussing present and revised
      criteria for determining rational suicide).

15   Tucker, *id.* at 1599, n. 23 (noting the American Medical Association's brief
      amicus curiae in Vacco and Glucksberg which endorsed the proper medical
      use of palliative sedation).
      Writing for the majority in Vacco, Chief Justice Rehnquist recognizes that
      a state may allow palliative care for patients refusing unwanted medical
      treatment "which may have the foreseen but unintended 'double effect' of
      hastening…death." 521 U.S. 793, 808, n. 11 (1997).
      But *see* David Orientleicher, *The Supreme Court and Terminal Sedation:
      Rejecting Suicide Embracing Euthanasia*, 24 HASTINGS CONST. L. Q. 947,
      955–56 (1997) (concluding terminal sedation is a form of active, voluntary or
      slow euthanasia).

16   Planned Parenthood of Southeastern Pa. v. Casey, 505 U.S. 833, 851 (1992)
      (Stevens, J.).

17   Kamisar, *supra* note 1 at 1474.

18   *Id.* at 1459.

19   *Id.* at 1471, 1472.

20   *Id.* at 1473.
      For Yale Kamisar, the supreme value of human life always trumps an exercise
      of autonomy or self-determination designed, as such, to end life. Yet,

DOI: 10.1057/9781137377395

interestingly, while he maintains that it is acceptable to honor a patient's wish to end an intolerably burdensome existence by ceasing medical treatment deemed futile, Kamisar would deny assistance to that individual to end his life. ROBERT YOUNG, MEDICALLY ASSISTED DEATH at 57 (2007). While Kamisar maintains further that a "critical moral significance" is to be found between an act and an omission, others assert the "distinction" between acts and omissions and between killing and letting die has no moral significance at all. YOUNG, *id.* at 56–8, Ch. 6. Callahan also characterizes the withdrawal of artificial nutrition and hydration as morally legitimate. Daniel Callahan, *Terminal Sedation and The Artefactual Fallacy*, in TERMINAL SEDATION: EUTHANASIA IN DISGUISE? at Ch. 9 (Torbjorn Tannsjo ed. 2004).

21 Kamisar, *supra* note 1 at 1471, 1472.
See Dan W. Brock, *Voluntary Active Euthanasia*, 22 HASTINGS CENTER RPT. 10, 14 (Mar.–April 1992).
The right to forego medical treatment is recognized as "virtually absolute" and in no way limited to the terminally ill. 1 ALAN MEISEL, THE RIGHT TO DIE §8.2 at 470 (2nd ed. 1995).
Since physicians have been permitted, legally, under the rubric of "forgoing life-sustaining treatment," to end the lives of the terminally ill for over 25 years, it becomes "a major hypocrisy" to perpetuate distinctions among the various *means* used to hasten death. No real difference can be drawn truthfully between "actively hastening death" and "passively hastening death." Alan Meisel, *Physician-Assisted Suicide: Shifting the Focus from Means to Ends*, at 283, 297 in PHYSICIAN-ASSISTED DYING: THE CASE FOR PALLIATIVE CARE AND PATIENT CHOICE (Timothy E. Quill and Margaret P. Battin eds. 2004).

22 Tucker, *supra* note 14 at 1610, n. 90 referencing the California Compassionate Choices Act introduced in 2007 which was not enacted into legislation.

23 ORE. REV. STAT. §§ 127.800 (12), 127.805 (2005).

24 Kamisar, *supra* note 1 at 1472.

25 *Id.*

26 *See* Adrienne M. Martin, *Hope and Exploitation*, 38 HASTINGS CENTER RPT. 49 (2008) (concluding hope should be viewed as a complex emotion which inputs value judgments and deliberative processes and—thus—should not be exploited to the point of being false or, at best, bereft of an accurate factual or scientific basis).

27 P-L Chau and Jonathan Herring, *The Meaning of Death*, in DEATH RITES AND RIGHTS Ch. 1 at 15 (Belinda Brooks-Gordon et al., eds. 2007). While patients in a PVS present with no level of cognition, those in a state of minimal consciousness have some level of cognitive function and a prognosis which is more open than for those in PVS and allows, as well, both

DOI: 10.1057/9781137377395

for transient and permanent recoveries. SHEPHERD, Ch. 4, *supra* note 79 at 22–3.

See J. T. Giacino et al., *The Minimally Conscious State: Definition and Diagnostic Criteria*, 58 NEUROLOGY 349 (2002).

See also Deborah Cook et al., *Withdrawal of Mechanical Ventilation in Anticipation of Death in the Intensive Care Unit*, 349 NEW ENG. J. MED. 1123 (Sept. 18, 2003).

28   SHEPHERD *id.*, at 145–46.

For patients in a PVS for six months, the probability of a recovery is 0%. Joshua E. Perry et al., *The Terri Schiavo Case: Legal, Ethical, and Medical Perspectives*, in BIOETHICS: AN INTRODUCTION TO THE HISTORY, METHODS, AND PRACTICE 400 at 402 (Nancy S. Jecker et al., eds. 2nd ed. 2007).

Individuals lacking higher brain functions (or being born without a brain as an anencephalic) and either permanently unconscious or insentient, should be considered dead. JANET L. DOLGIN and LOIS L. SHEPHERD, BIOETHICS AND THE LAW 842–48 (2nd ed. 2009).

29   *Supra*, Ch. 4, n's 66–90 and accompanying text.

30   Chau and Herring, *supra* note 27.

31   *Id.*

32   Chau and Herring, *supra* note 27 at 19.

33   *Id.*

34   *Id.*

See President's Council on Bioethics, *Controversies in the Determination of Death: White Paper* (2008) for a full analysis of opposing positions within the medico-legal and philosophical communities on the accuracy and validity of using a (preferred) neurological standard for reaching a clinical determination of "whole brain death."

35   *See* Richard A. McCormick, SJ, *"To Save or Let Die: The Dilemma of Modern Medicine,"* 229 JAMA 172 (1974).

36   *See generally* SHEPHERD, *supra* note 27; THE CASE OF TERRI SCHIAVO: ETHICS AT THE END OF LIFE (Arthur L. Caplan, James J. McCartney, and Dominic A. Sisti eds. 2006).

37   SHEPHERD, *supra* note 27 at 174.

38   SHEPHERD, *supra* note 27; BARRY R. SCHALLER, UNDERSTANDING BIOETHICS AND THE LAW (2008).

Terri's parents argued that she was not in a PVS, but rather minimally conscious. SHEPHERD, *supra* note 27 at 22–3. Under either condition, Terri should not have been fed by hand or otherwise. SHEPHERD, *supra* note 27 at 11.

39   SCHALLER, *id.* at 160.

DOI: 10.1057/9781137377395

See Annette Rid and David Windler, *Can We Improve Treatment Decision-Making for Incapacitated Patients?*, 40 HASTINGS CENTER RPT. 36 (2010).

40 *Id.*
    See George J. Annas, *Culture of Life Politics at the Bedside—The Cases of Terri Schiavo*, 352 NEW ENG. J. MED. 1710 (2005); Symposium, *Reflections and Implications of Schiavo*, 35 STETSON L. REV. 1 (2005).

41 SCHALLER, *id.* at Ch. 7.

42 *Id.*; SHEPHERD, *supra* note 27.
    The principal legal documents, together with the time-line, for the Terri Schiavo case may be found at <http://www6.miami.edu/ethics/schiavo/terri_schiavo_timeline.html>.

43 SHEPHERD, *supra* note 27 at 186.
    Sadly, Terri Schiavo's parents thought that—medically and legally—she should be viewed as one suffering from a disability rather than being in a futile medical condition and dying. Loane Skene, *The Schiavo and Korp Cases: Conceptualizing End-of-Life Decision-making*, 13 J. L. & MED. 223, 224–25 (2005).

44 The original Directive 58 was issued in 2001.
    Directive 58, Ethical and Religious Directions for Catholic Health Care Services. *See supra* Ch. 4, note 77.
    See Sandra Johnson, *The Catholic Bishops, the Law, and Nutrition and Hydration: An Historical Footnote*, 19 ANNALS HEALTH L. 97 (2010).

45 Johnson, *id.* at 98.

46 *Id.*
    See Alan Sanders, *The Clinical Reality of Artificial Nutrition ad Hydration for Patients at The End of Life*, 9 NAT'L CATH. BIOETHICS Q. 293, 304 (2009). *See generally* ARTIFICIAL NUTRITION AND HYDRATION: THE NEW CATHOLIC DEBATE (Christopher Tollefsen ed. 2008).

47 Johnson, *supra* note 44 at 98.
    But see generally Kevin D. O'Rourke, OP, *When to Withdraw Support*, 8 NAT'L CATH. BIOETHICS Q. 663, 671 (2008) (observing "prolonging life is not an absolute mandate"); John H. Connery, *Prolonging Life: The Duty and Its Limits*, 47 LINACRE Q. 151 (1980).

48 *See* Kathleen Boozang, *An Intimate Passing: Restoring the Role of Family and Religion in Dying*, 58 U. PITT. L. REV. 549 (1997).
    See generally GEORGE P. SMITH, II, THE CHRISTIAN RELIGION AND BIOTECHNOLOGY: A SEARCH FOR PRINCIPLED DECISION-MAKING (2005).

49 Boozang, *id.* at 611.

50 *Id.* at 598.

51 *Id.*

DOI: 10.1057/9781137377395

52 Stewart Eskew and Christopher Meyers, *Religious Beliefs and Surrogate Decision Making*, 20 J. CLIN. ETHICS 192, 195 (2009).

53 ROBERT AUDI, RELIGIOUS COMMITMENT AND SECULAR REASON 86 *passim* (2000).

54 Robert S. Olick et al., *Accommodating Religious and Moral Objections to Neurological Death*, 20 J. CLIN. ETHICS 183, 187 (2009).

55 *Id.*

56 *Id.* at 188–89.

57 *Id.* at 189.

58 381 U.S. 479 (1965).

59 405 U.S. 438 (1972).

60 539 U.S. 558 (2003).

61 *Id.*

62 539 U.S. 558, 564–65.

63 *Id.*

64 Kamisar, *supra* note 1 at 1466.

65 *Id.*

66 Planned Parenthood of Se. Pa. v. Casey, 505 U.S. 833, 847 (1992), (O'Connor, J. Kennedy, J. and Souter, J.).
    See Daniel E. Lee, *Physician-Assisted Suicide: A Conservative Critique of Intervention*, 33 HASTINGS CENTER RPT. 17 (2003).

67 *See* DAVID C. THOMASMA and GLENN C. GRABER, EUTHANASIA: TOWARD AN ETHICAL SOCIAL POLICY Ch. 2 (1991).

68 Cruzan v. Dir., Mo. Dep't Health, 497 U.S. 261 (1990).
    Artificial alimentation (e.g., nourishment) and hydration are not readily distinguishable "from other forms of medical treatment," and, as such, can be refused by a competent patient exercising his "liberty interest" in refusing such treatments. 497 U.S. at 287–88 (1990) (O'Connor, J. concurring).

69 Erwin Chemerinsky, *Washington v. Glucksberg Was Tragically Wrong*, 106 MICH. L. REV. 1501 (2008); DANIEL CALLAHAN, THE TROUBLED DREAM OF LIFE 107–08 (1993).

70 FURROW et al., *supra* Ch. 4, note 4 at 43.

71 *Id.*
    Indeed, some twenty-one states have these pain relief laws and seven states allow specifically for use of medical marijuana. For a complete listing of the state statutes, *see*: http://www.painandthelaw.org/statutes/statepainacts.php.
    Interestingly, the federal government has been unsuccessful in enacting pain and relief legislation which would allow the presumption of controlled substances in order to manage refractory pain. *See* the Pain Relief Promotion Act (H.R. 3360) (2005) and S. 1272 (1999).
    See generally Campell and Cox, *supra* Ch. 1, note 51.

DOI: 10.1057/9781137377395

72 Yale Kamisar, *Are the Distinctions Drawn in the Debate about End-of-Life Decision Making "Principled"? If Not, How Much Does it Matter?*, 40 J. L. MED. & ETHICS 66, 79 (2012).

73 *Id.*
See generally, George P. Smith, II, *Quality of Life, Sanctity of Creation: Palliative or Apotheosis?*, 63 NEB. L. REV. 709 (1984).

74 Kamisar, *id.* (referencing GUIDO CALABRESI and PHILIP BOBBITT, TRAGIC CHOICES at 17–19, 57–8 (1978)).

75 Kamisar, *id.* at 79.

76 Meisel, *supra* note 21.

77 *See generally*, PELLEGRINO and THOMASMA, *supra* Ch. 1, note 70.

6
Shaping a Compassionate Response to End-stage Illness

Abstract: *This chapter examines the degree to which caring responses should be integral to the ideal of a just society. If such a response is accepted as an ethic of care or viewed as a "right" to "responsible benevolence" at the end-stage of life, the goal of the law should be to accommodate—to the degree possible—a dignified death. Indeed, safeguarding the notion of death with dignity and assuring minimal discomfort and pain in the process is of paramount interest to the state—especially since the duty to relieve pain and suffering is recognized as the least disputed and most universal of the moral obligations health care providers, as licensed by the state, must honor.*

George P. Smith. *Palliative Care and End-of-Life Decisions.* New York: Palgrave Macmillan, 2013.
DOI: 10.1057/9781137377395.

Caring, as a role and obligation for health care providers, may be seen as a moral obligation rooted in the time-honored principle of beneficence whose goal is to promote patient well-being.[1] Considered as such, "caring indubitably incorporates empathy."[2] Incorporating it into the management of the terminally ill is, however, difficult. For the physician to convey to a patient that "I *could* be you," involves a sympathetic response which—ideally—may be initiated during the taking of the patient history.[3] During this process, a one-on-one relationship may be commenced which provides a mechanism for physician assessment and identification of the emotion the terminally ill patient is experiencing, a determination of the reason for the display of emotion and then a response to the patient which allows him, the patient, to see that a "connection" has been made by the physician between the emotion and its root cause.[4] A line of communication is then opened.

Establishment of an empathetic response by the physician also has the direct effect of assuring that the patient will not be abandoned in his final days. For many physicians, however, non-abandonment is difficult—instinctively—to honor because of "the fear generated by confrontation of their own mortality when caring for a dying patient."[5] Because of this situation, patient avoidance—unintentional though it may be—only serves to heighten patient fears of impending death.[6]

Because of these concerns and inadequacies among physicians, more often than not, issues of existential care are left to the nursing staff.[7] And, even in the daily hospital bed environment, it takes a special level of sensitivity for the nursing staff to understand questions often raised indirectly by the patients regarding the depth and severity of their distress over their terminal illness. Once understood, it remains for the nurses to devise a procedure for providing empathetic support.[8]

Alleviating suffering

While autonomy emerged in the 20th century as the dominant or capstone principle in biomedical ethics—supporting and complementing beneficence, non-malfeasance, and distributive justice[9]—it is well to re-consider its pre-eminence in complex cases of refractory pain. Indeed, once cases are presented where one's quality of life is so severe and diminished because of suffering, it is proper to advance an argument which necessitates a re-configuring or enhancement of autonomy so that

DOI: 10.1057/9781137377395

compassion becomes the operative bioethical principle in decisionmaking at this level.[10] Accordingly, in case scenarios where end-of-life pain is intractable, efforts to address this condition and thereby assure a dignified death become a paramount state interest.

The goal of alleviating suffering, if acknowledged as a *right* to relief, requires action by the state and the health care providers and imposes upon them a co-ordinate responsibility to make prudential judgments which validate this right.[11] Honoring or, indeed, acknowledging such a right then becomes an act of "responsible benevolence"[12] and is seen properly as complementing the duty to undertake actions which benefit the dying patient.[13] The duty to relieve pain is acknowledged as the "least disputed and most universal of the moral obligations of the physician."[14] In reality, end-of-life autonomy is actually fortified by and through this new right of compassion. Of necessity, compassion then becomes the denominator in health care decisions for end-of-life care[15] and directs that efforts should be undertaken which not only refrain from causing pain or suffering but—as well—relieve it.[16]

Legal caring responses in a just society

American history shows rather remarkably that instead of being perceived as vital to maintenance of a just society, the capacity to care has been often seen as antithetical to it.[17] As a consequence of this attitude, there " has been a deformation of both the private ethic care and the very public ethic of legal justices."[18] This, in turn, has meant that not only have ideals and practices of justice been uncaring, but the ideals and practices of care "have been unjust" with a "deflation of both values" resulting.[19] Rather than viewing care giving as an emotional, morally arbitrary response, it should be more properly accepted as an ethical activity—with the beliefs and values of care accepted as "integral to development of a just society."[20] Indeed, care or compassion must be recognized as a universal moral principle[21] which is vital to the very fabric of social justice.[22]

Within every adjudication, it has been suggested that neutral principles of law, or those standards which transcend the instant case, should operate.[23] Perhaps these principles or standards are to be found within the very principle of equity;[24] and from equity flows arguably, mercy, sympathy, compassion, humaneness or love.[25] David Hume, an 18th

DOI: 10.1057/9781137377395

century British philosopher, opined that the basis for a system of justice and social solidarity was, in fact, tied to expressions of natural sympathy for others.[26] Arthur Schopenhauer, the German philosopher, maintained that compassion "is the real basis of all voluntary justice."[27] Accordingly, for an action to have moral value, it must derive from compassion.[28]

Defined as an acknowledgment of another's suffering which prompts a response to assist in alleviating the suffering, compassion is often regarded as the motivation for subsequent merciful acts.[29] Mercy is oftentimes used synonymously with compassion or benevolence.[30] Indeed, acts of this nature have been termed "responsible benevolence,"[31] or "compassionate mercy."[32]

For others, charity is seen as the ultimate value in caring for the dying;[33] and they suggest beneficence and benevolence may combine, properly, to become "loving charity."[34] When there is suffering, its elimination or management is central and can well be seen as trumping the biomedical principle of autonomy.[35]

Modernly, it has been urged that sympathy and compassion must be integrated into contemporary law.[36] A modern and principled rule of law, then, needs notions of decency and compassion within its sinews[37] and does not have to conflict with a rule of love.[38] Others have called for the law to be empathetic which is used often, interchangeably, with love, altruism, and sympathy.[39]

One of the inherent weaknesses of the rule of law has been said to be its all-too-often efforts to distance itself from human experience.[40] Certainly by introducing human values or attitudes into the judicial process a strong claim could be made that they might well conflict with the ideal of judging which is sustained by rational and objective argumentation and not feelings and emotions.[41] Indeed, empathetic discourse may well be seen as either irrelevant or merely policy and, thus, dismissed.[42]

Principles, emotions, and the Holmesian Caveat

While principles provide the foundational framework for standards of normative conduct, feelings are important when individuals or *micro* issues arise which, in turn, test the extent to which principles are valid in their application within the context of a given situation or norm of conduct.[43] It is asserted that "the morally good person is just not principled, but also compassionate."[44] As well, that person not only exhibits "practical

DOI: 10.1057/9781137377395

wisdom"[45] but "simple common sense"[46] in assuring that patient dignity or quality of life is preserved throughout all palliative care treatments.[47]

The best way to assure this mandate or goal throughout cases of adjusted palliative care management is to embrace a test of medical utility in determining what end-stage options should be made available as treatment.[48] Accordingly, a benefits to burdens/risk calculus should be utilized to assess the utility of one medical treatment over another.[49] Anchoring such an evaluation should be the doctrine of medical futility which acknowledges the practical limits of medical treatment in all cases.[50]

While compassion is experienced and evaluated subjectively,[51] it need not stigmatize a valid legal theory.[52] Indeed, in the case of *De Shaney v. Winnebago County Dept. of Social Services* et al.,[53] Justice Harry Blackmun, in dissent, addressed the importance of compassion in judicial analysis and interpretation by observing "…compassion need not be exiled from the province of judging."[54] He went further and stated that when "'natural sympathy'" is removed from a case by courts, they are thereby prevented "from recognizing the facts of the case before it or the legal norms that should apply to those facts."[55]

Eschewing emotion as a dominant vector of force in truth seeking in law,[56] Oliver Wendell Holmes, Jr. urged that the reasoning behind a particular rule's adoption "ought to be of paramount importance."[57] And, when the reasons for structuring the rule have disappeared, it is improper to maintain the rule, "from blind imitation of the past."[58] Indeed, Judge Richard Posner has observed that when conventional sources of judicial guidance are scant or have been exhausted, judges will often not be "centrally concerned with securing consistency with past enactments."[59] Instead, care will be taken to produce "the best results for the future."[60] This type of pragmatic adjudication (derived from legal pragmatism), then, places a "heightened judicial concern for consequences and thus a disposition to base policy judgments on them rather than on conceptualisms and generalities."[61]

Surely, the reasons behind the prohibitions and restricted use of terminal sedation as a means of care in palliative treatment of patients in end-stage care need to be, at minimum, re-evaluated and even expanded to include such care of patients suffering severe psychological distress in illnesses of this type. Suffering at the end-of-life may be manifested in different forms—in presenting with physical symptomology—of psychological, emotional and existential suffering as either despair, feelings

DOI: 10.1057/9781137377395

of helplessness an isolation or a basic loss of self respect.[62] And, as seen, a right not to suffer must be acknowledged,[63] together with a professional responsibility among physicians to validate this right—to the extent that they can undersound medical practice—alleviate the suffering.

A contemporary model in legal decisionmaking

The law should accord a greater "caring response"[64] or a "sense of shared humanity"[65] in its interpretation and application. This value, and others of equal merit, are essential to sustaining the rule of law.[66] Oftentimes, however, values are challenged or perceived as being in conflict with abstruse "moralistic abstractions about liberty, equality and dignity."[67]

Unquestionably, decisions in health care concerning the maintenance of life and the hastening of death often pose complicated moral questions which are anchored in normative reasoning which—in turn—may, or may not, be relevant or cogent because of changing contemporary values.[68] If moral reasoning is either ambiguous or ineffectual, courts will rely on "moral intuitions," or "assumptions about intrinsic normative order" found implicitly "in the natural course of life."[69] Analytical frameworks of this nature invite conflict because of non-verifiable subjective values—this, because determining normative assumptions which animate moral judgments is very difficult if not indiscernible.[70]

In order to add order or greater precision in their analyses, courts can choose to embrace the philosophy of Holmes—as seen—which prizes logic over experience.[71] By adhering to legal formalism, moral judgments are avoided altogether[72]—this, in very large part because there is an awareness that it is very difficult to safeguard and sustain social solidarity if emotional values are given recognition in the processes of judicial decisionmaking.[73] If, however, formalism is rejected, judicial deference can then be given to "tradition and convention"[74] as a construct for discerning moral convictions or discovering shared humanity instead of a rigid adherence to "academic reasoning."[75]

The best approach to or model for judicial decisionmaking is one that achieves a balance between logical reasoning and, when appropriate, "critical morality" as opposed to traditional conventional morality.[76] As such, the courts must endeavor to apply a situation ethic rather than an unyielding and rigid normative standard[77] and to then proceed to acknowledge love or *agape* as the controlling moral principle in all

DOI: 10.1057/9781137377395

judicial decisionmaking. Stated otherwise, guided by compassion or humaneness, the judiciary should interpret ever evolving social values and the social conditions which shape those values.[78] Of necessity, these values and conditions change with the facts of each case and, thus, so also does the extent to which compassion and humaneness are pertinent. The ultimate goal of judicial decisionmaking should, in the final analysis, be a "practical realization of the rule of law."[79]

Notes

1   Paul Rousseau, *The Fears of Death and The Physician's Responsibility to Care for the Dying*, 18 AM. J. HOSP. & PALLIATIVE CARE 224 (July–Aug. 2001). *See generally* JONATHAN HERRING, CARING AND THE LAW (2013).
2   Rousseau, *id.*
3   *Id.* at 225.
4   *Id.*
5   *Id..*
6   *Id.*
     See END-OF-LIFE ISSUES, GRIEF AND BEREAVEMENT (Sara H. Qualls and Julia E. Kaal-Godley eds. 2011).
7   Robert Hoatpen and David Hendrikx, *Nurses and The Vicissitudes of Dealing with Euthanasia Questions in Terminal Palliative Care*, 10 NURSING ETHICS 377 (2003).
8   *Id*
     But see Leeat Granek, *When Doctors Grieve*, N.Y. TIMES, May 27, 2012 at 12. (noting the real struggle that oncologists have to manage their feelings of grief when their patients succumb with the detachment necessary to be objective in their work as physicians).
9   *See* ALBERT R. JONSEN, *A History of Bioethics and Discipline and Discourse*, in BIOETHICS: AN INTRODUCTION TO THE HISTORY, METHODS, AND PRACTICE 3–22 (Nancy C. Jecker et al., eds. 2007).
     See generally GEORGE P. SMITH, II, BIOETHICS AND THE LAW: MEDICAL, SOCIO-LOCAL AND PHILOSOPHICAL DIRECTIONS FOR A BRAVE NEW WORLD (1993).
10   Shepherd, Ch. 2, *supra* note 9 at 147.
11   *Id.* at 146.
     See Symposium: Health Law and The Elderly: Managing Risk at The End of Life, 17 WIDENER L. REV. 347 (2011).
12   LIEZL VAN ZYL, DEATH AND COMPASSION: A VIRTUE BASED APPROACH TO EUTHANASIA 197 (2000).

DOI: 10.1057/9781137377395

13 THOMASMA and GRABER, *supra* Ch. 5, note 67.
See RICHARD EPSTEIN, MORTAL PERIL 304–05 (1999) (asserting that consenting terminally ill patients "need" to be allowed or assisted to end their lives whenever "a rational agent could prefer death to life."). Margaret Battin has suggested nonvoluntary euthanasia should be available to those medical patients who do not have a "realistic desire" for continued care—for, it is an "act of injustice" to maintain those unable to enjoy a basic quality of life. Individuals of this type would include those who are "permanently comatose, decerebrate, profoundly brain damaged, and others who lack cognitive function." MARGARET P. BATTIN, *infra* Ch. 7, note 29 at 120–21.

14 THOMAS and GRABER, *supra* Ch. 5, note 67 at 194 (quoting Dr. Edmund D. Pellegrino).
See Shawna E. Oyoba, *Holding Hawaii Nursing Facilities Accountable for the Inadequate Pain Management of Elderly Residents*, 27 U. HAW. L. REV. 223, 244 at n. 103 (2004) (observing that failing to treat pain can amount to elder abuse).

15 THOMAS and GRABER, *id.* at 126.

16 MARGARET P. BATTIN, ENDING LIFE: ETHICS AND THE WAY WE DIE 90, 91 (2005).

17 ROBIN WEST, CARING FOR JUSTICE 7, 9 (1997).
See MICHAEL FINE, A CARING SOCIETY Ch. 3 (2007).

18 WEST, *id.* at 9.
See JONATHAN HERRING, OLDER PEOPLE IN LAW AND SOCIETY 127 (2009).

19 WEST, *id.*

20 FINE, *supra* note 17 at 63; HERRING, *supra* note 18 at 125–27.
See Knauer, *supra* Ch. 1, note 8.

21 FINE, *id.* at 61; JONSEN, *supra* Ch. 5, note 65 at 126.

22 *See generally* MARIAN BARNES, CARING AND SOCIAL JUSTICE Ch. 8 (2006).

23 Herbert Wechsler, *Toward Neutral Principles of Law*, 73 HARV. L. REV. 1, 17, 29 (1959).

24 *See generally* WILLIAM Q. DeFUNIAK, HANDBOOK ON MODERN EQUITY, Ch. 1 (2nd ed. 1956); Garrard Glenn and Kenneth Redden, *Equity: A Visit to the Founding Fathers*, 31 VA. L. REV. 753, 756 (1945) (quoting Blackstone's idea that "equity exists for corrections of situations wherein the law, by reason of its universality, is deficient.").

25 Equity is defined as not only "the quality of being equal or fair ..." but, "given in accordance with natural justice... something fair and right." V OXFORD ENGLISH DICTIONARY 358 (2nd ed. 1989).

26 Paul T. Menzel, *Justice and the Basic Structure of Health Care Systems* in MEDICINE AND SOCIAL JUSTICE at 261, 262 (Rosamund Rhodes, Margaret P. Battin and Anita Silvers ed. 2002).

DOI: 10.1057/9781137377395

27   WILLIAM S. SAHAKIAN and MABEL LEWIS SAHAKIAN, IDEAS OF THE GREAT PHILOSOPHERS 49 (1993).

28   *Id.*

29   Steven Tudor, *Modes of Mercy*, 28 AUSTRALIAN J. LEGAL PHIL. 79, 95 (2003).
      See also Patrick Guinan, *The Christian Origin of Medical Compassion*, 5 NAT'L CATHOLIC BIOETHICS Q. 21 (2005); Martha C. Nussbaum, *Compassion: The Basic Social Emotion*, 13 SOC. PHIL. & POL'Y 27 (1996).

30   Tudor, *id.* at 81.

31   VAN ZYL, *supra* note 12 at 197.

32   BATTIN, *supra* note 16 at 66.
      See also TIMOTHY E. QUILL, DEATH AND DIGNITY: MAKING CHOICES AND TAKING CHARGE 131 *passim* (1994).

33   Edmund D. Pellegrino, *Decision at The End of Life: The Use and Abuse of The Concept of Futility*, in THE DIGNITY OF THE DYING PERSON 231 (Juan De Dios Vial Correa and Elio Segreccia eds. 2000).

34   *Id.* at 225, 241.

35   Shepherd, *supra* note 10 at 106, 119.

36   Laurence Tribe, *Revisiting the Rule of Law*, 64 N.Y.U. L. REV. 726, 729 (1989).

37   *Id.* at 731.

38   *Id.* at 729.
      See JOHN FLETCHER, SITUATION ETHICS: THE NEW MORALITY (1966) (where the argument is presented which holds that so long as one's intention to act is anchored in love, the end result justifies the means). For Fletcher, the Situation Ethic is a variant or sub-set of moral ethics which, in turn, holds ethics are relative to culture, immediate circumstances and specific individual needs. *See generally* SAMUEL FLEISCHACKER, INTEGRITY AND MORAL RELATIVISM (1992), HUGH LaFOLLETTE, THE TRUTH IN ETHICAL RELATIVISM (where an argument is advanced which eschews routine application of existing moral rules and stresses, instead, that a "cultivated moral judgment" should be the normative standard of conduct).

39   Lynne N. Henderson, *Legality and Empathy*, 85 MICH. L. REV. 1574, 1579–82 (1987).
      See RICHARD A. POSNER, HOW JUDGES THINK 117 (2008) (observing that an element of "good judgment" in judicial decisionmaking is "empathy" and "common sense").
      But see David Brooks, *The Limits of Empathy* N.Y. TIMES, Sept. 30, 2011, at A21 (referencing one current study which found empathy "subverts justice" because its display is keyed to emotionalism rather than pragmatism and objectivity and—furthermore—provides a way "to experience the illusion of moral progress without having to do the nasty work of making moral judgments").

DOI: 10.1057/9781137377395

40 *See generally* JOHN NOONAN, PERSONS AND MASKS OF THE LAW (1976).

41 Benjamin Zipursky, *De Shaney and The Jurisprudence of Compassion*, 65 N.Y.U.L. REV. 1101, 1122 (1990).
But see MARTIN L. HOFFMAN, EMPATHY AND MORAL DEVELOPMENT: IMPLICATIONS FOR CARING AND JUSTICE (2000).

42 Henderson, *supra* note 39 at 1588.
See generally LOU AGOSTA, EMPATHY IN THE CONTEXT OF PHILOSOPHY (2010); FRANS De WAAL, THE AGE OF EMPATHY (2009); Brooks, *supra* note 39.

43 RANDALL and DOWNIE, *supra* Ch. 1, note 17 at 12–13.

44 *Id.* at 13.

45 *Id.* at 24.

46 *Id.* at 73.

47 Annette F. Street and David W. Kissane, *Constructions of Dignity in End-of-Life Care*, 17 J. PALLIATIVE CARE 93, 95, 99 (2001).

48 RANDALL and DOWNIE, *supra* Ch. 1, note 17 at Ch. 1.

49 *Id.* at 116–18.

50 *Id.*

51 Zipursky, *supra* note 41 at 1142.

52 *Id.* at 1147.
See Lois L. Shepherd, *Face to Face: A Call for Radical Responsibility in Place of Compassion*, 77 ST. JOHN'S L. REV. 444 at 449, 457 (2003) (calling for a greater prominence for caring responses in law and a sense of "shared humanity").

53 489 U.S. 189 (1988).

54 *Id.* at 213.

55 *Id.*

56 OLIVER WENDELL HOLMES, JR., THE ESSENTIAL HOLMES: SELECTIONS FROM THE LETTERS, SPEECHES, JUDICIAL OPINIONS, AND OTHER WRITINGS OF OLIVER WENDELL HOLMES, Jr. at 119 (Richard A. Posner ed. 1992).

57 Oliver Wendell Holmes, Jr., *The Path of The Law*, 10 HARV. L. REV. 457 (1987).
See RICHARD A. POSNER, LAW, PRAGMATISM AND DEMOCRACY 107 (2003) (arguing ordinary people have little interest in complex policy and—with half of the population with I.Q's of below 100—limited intellectual depth).

58 *Id.*
See generally MAGNUSSON, *supra* Ch. 2, note 42; Stephen W. Smith, *Some Realism about End of Life: The Current Prohibition and The Euthanasia Underground*, 33 AM. J. L. & MED. 55 (2007).

59 RICHARD A. POSNER, THE PROBLEMATICS OF MORAL AND LEGAL THEORY 24 (1989).

DOI: 10.1057/9781137377395

60   *Id.*

61   POSNER, *supra* note 39 at 228 (2008).
     See generally RICHARD A. POSNER, OVERCOMING LAW (1995);
     RICHARD A POSNER, THE PROBLEMS OF JURISPRUDENCE (1990).

62   VAN ZYL, *supra* note 12 at 196.

63   THOMASMA and GRABER, *supra* Ch. 1, note 70 at 192.

64   Shepherd, *supra* note 52 at 449.

65   *Id.* at 457.

66   Neil S. Siegel, *The Virtue of Judicial Statesmanship*, 86 TEX. L. REV. 961, 971
     (2008).
     See Edmund Ursin, *How Great Judges: Judges Richard Posner, Henry Friendly,
     and Roger Traynor on Judicial Lawmaking*, 57 BUFF L. REV. 1267 (2009).

67   Siegel, *id.* at 1030.

68   Steven D. Smith, *De-Moralized: Glucksberg in The Malaise*, 106 MICH. L. REV.
     1571, 1589 (2008).

69   *Id.* at 1589–90.

70   *Id.* at 1590.

71   Holmes, *supra* note 56.

72   Smith, *supra* note 68 at 1590.

73   *See generally* Cass R. Sunstein, *Due Process Traditionalism*, 106 MICH. L. REV.
     1543 (2008); Siegel, *supra* note 66 at 979.
     See also WILLIAM F. SULLIVAN, EYE OF THE HEART: KNOWING THE
     HUMAN GOOD IN THE EUTHANASIA DEBATE Ch. 2 (2005).

74   Smith, *supra* note 68 at 1590.

75   *Id.*

76   *Id.*
     Judge Richard Posner suggests that by employing a type of reasoning termed,
     "cultural cognition," which is considered "a valid though flawed sense of
     knowledge," a judge is allowed to consider his personal vision of those
     policies important to him in order to advance his model of a good society.
     "The personal, the emotional and the intuitive" are factors used in judicial
     making—with the intuitive being a real factor in appellate review. POSNER,
     supra note 39 at 116, 117.

77   *See generally* FLETCHER, *supra* note 38.

78   Siegel, *supra* note 66 at 981.

79   *Id.* at 979.
     See generally, George P. Smith, II, *Judicial Decisionmaking in the Age of
     Biotechnology*, 13 NOTRE DAME J. LAW ETHICS & PUB. POLICY 34 (1999).

DOI: 10.1057/9781137377395

7

Toward a Good Death: A Socio-legal, Ethical, and Medical Challenge

Abstract: *This chapter recapitulates the positive steps being taken incrementally to promote and ensure that either an ethic or a right to a compassionate death is evolving. The salutary effect of the Uniform Health Care Act in establishing parameters for determining medical futility—taken together with the efforts of the Academy of Palliative Medicine to structure standards for regulating nutrition and hydration in palliative management—and the guidance of the American Medical Association in establishing when it is clinically and ethically proper to sedate to unconsciousness, are powerful paradigms evidencing a new movement toward shaping contemporary standards of normative conduct for end-of-life decision making. Of necessity, these standards are grounded in notions of compassion, dignity, beneficence and common sense.*

George P. Smith. *Palliative Care and End-of-Life Decisions.* New York: Palgrave Macmillan, 2013.
DOI: 10.1057/9781137377395.

Patient values must always be viewed as the base line for developing and pursuing patient-centered palliative care for terminal illness.[1] Best patient care, then, is adjusted—of necessity—to a patient's changing medical condition.[2] Palliative care provides adjusted care by endeavoring to relieve end-stage suffering of all kinds[3]—physical and psychological. If this is seen or recognized as a right to relief from suffering,[4] as the European Federation for Pain Study advocates,[5] then heath care providers and the state have a basic responsibility to establish policies designed to validate the right to avoid suffering and follow a course of action which seeks to honor the wants and desires of patients for a dignified death.[6] Indeed, as observed, there is a medical duty to act to benefit the dying by relieving pain.[7] Accordingly, both law and medicine must set standards or protocols which allow for the wider adoption and use of terminal sedation as an efficacious and humane practice for end-stage care of patients in hospice.[8]

Efforts to accept, and then adopt, a protocol for specifically determining medical futility[9] will be enhanced and legitimized by a wider adoption of the Uniform Health Care Decisions Act.[10] The works of the American Academy of Palliative Medicine to develop, and thereby structure, standards for regulating nutrition and hydration in palliative management,[11] together with the American Medical Association's guidance on when, clinically and ethically, it is proper to sedate to unconsciousness,[12] are having a salutary effect on both codifying and—thus—stabilizing proper medical care and procedures in end-of-life care. Significant progress is also seen by Rosseau in proposing a protocol for the administration of palliative or terminal sedation[13] and by Morita[14] and Quill.[15] In addition to providing a framework for principled decisionmaking in end-stage care these actions serve to educate the public to the parameters of appropriate medical care and humane treatment for the terminally ill.[16]

Once a new codified framework or template for decisionmaking emerges, an informed dialogue can begin anew which addresses itself to one question: namely, is the terminally ill individual exercising rational thinking in his treatment decisions which, in turn, validate self-determination or autonomy?[17] Alternatively, when he is deemed incompetent to make end-of-life decision, the issue becomes whether the healthcare provider is not only acting consistent with standard medical practice,[18] but is endeavoring to make a "value consequent choice"—consistent with the patient's values[19] and thus within the best interests of the terminal patient.[20] Independent of any prior patient request,

DOI: 10.1057/9781137377395

treatment withdrawals and significant drug dosages are "standard medical practices that are routinely justified as being in the best interests of patients who lack capacity to express their own views."[21]

Ultimately, determining the parameters of a patient's best medical interests are shaped by policies of reasonableness[22] and compassion.[23] As seen, reasonableness is not capable of a precise formulation, but—rather—is tied inextricably to issues of proportionality or cost/benefit analysis[24] which, in turn, must remain fact-sensitive and shaped by the "accepted standards of medical practice" applicable within each medical case presented.[25]

The popular notion within the American society that there is a required prescription to treat under all circumstances, needs to be re-evaluated and brought into contemporary focus through acceptance of the doctrine of medical futility.[26] Under this recognized doctrine, as seen, when medical care is complemented by the test of proportionality imbedded presently in the principle of double effect, the central treatment question becomes whether the burdens of treatment clearly outweigh its benefits to the patient and would be inhumane if continued.[27] In those cases where medical treatment is seen as futile, terminal sedation should be recognized as but a part of end-stage total symptom management—and validated as an integral part of palliative management. Once at the end-stage, terminal suffering is managed more effectively, the law must change the legal taxonomy and reliance on the principle of double effect in testing whether assistance in ending life is capital murder or euthanasia. Instead, the degree of necessity for providing compassionate assistance to dying patients—together with an assessment of the soundness of the medical judgment of the healthcare providers rendering the assistance, should be pivotal in legal analysis of end-stage care. Indeed, the central or fundamental part of the end-of-life equation for making rational medical decisions must always be seen as the patient's quest for a dignified death[28] or, alternatively, the "least worst death."[29] A good death is said, commonly, to be one which occurs "after a long and successful life, at home, without violence or pain, with the dying person being at peace with his environment and having at least some control over events."[30]

Rather than continue the quest to establish a constitutional right to assisted suicide, perhaps—in the final analysis—the time-honored common law of the right to refuse treatment should be seen as the corner stone for building a more compassionate and enlightened ethic of

DOI: 10.1057/9781137377395

understanding in managing end-of-life issues.[31] This right of refusal is not a right to hasten death—but, rather, merely a right to resist physical invasions which are unwanted.[32]

With the passage of the Patient Self-Determination Act by Congress in 1990,[33] a bold first step was taken which served as a national legislative validation of the right to refuse treatment.[34] As seen, this legislation strengthened patient autonomy by allowing newly admitted hospital and nursing home patients to choose whether they wished to either accept or refuse specified medical treatment during the course of their confinement.[35]

Additional steps in building an arsenal to safeguard a framework for principled decisionmaking in end-of-life cases were taken by the development of the Uniform Health Care Decisions Act,[36] the successful efforts of some states to enact pain-relief statutes,[37] the Death with Dignity statutes of Oregon,[38] Vermont and Washington,[39] and the medical protocols for use of palliative (hospice) care and terminal sedation.[40] These "weapons" in the arsenal serve to protect and encourage sound, reasonable medical judgments and—thus—in a very real way, balance physicians powers and protections with patient rights of autonomy.

Utility, most assuredly, comes into play after medical conditions are assessed and evaluated and a treatment prognosis is charted.[41] It is within the boundaries of utility that the principle of medical futility is indeed tested and determined to be efficacious or, as to a particular case, invalid. Cost/benefit (or, simply proportional) analysis of treatment benefits is central to a determination of medical futility since[42]—first and foremost—this is but a clinical judgment and not an encompassing moral pronouncement or principle on the "worthlessness" of a life.[43] Whether the operable normative standard for policymaking be termed *agape*,[44] charity,[45] compassion,[46] love,[47] or mercy,[48] the common or unifying denominator of palliative care is a humane, morally responsible approach to dealing with intractable suffering at the end-stage of life.

Good judgment is to be expected of judicial decision makers just as it is for healthcare providers. As a quality in reasoning, good judgment is characterized as "an elusive compound of *empathy*, modesty, maturity, a sense of proportion, balance, a recognition of human limitations, sanity, prudence, a sense of reality and *common sense*."[49] Elusive though such judgment may be to capture or own, sound, reasoned judgments in medico-legal decisionmaking must be the norm and not the exception.

DOI: 10.1057/9781137377395

To initiate or continue with medical treatment which is determined to be medically futile should be recognized as simply wrong; for acting in such a manner, not only denies the fact of human finitude but, additionally, it imposes unnecessary effort, expense and emotional trauma on both patient and other affected parties.[50] As well, when efforts to treat futile medical conditions are undertaken, such actions serve as a total abnegation of one of the cardinal principles of medical ethics—namely beneficence.[51]

It has been argued persuasively that while the state may declare a legitimate interest in morality,[52] for it to meet a heightened level of judicial scrutiny on review of such end-of-life declarations, it faces an increasingly difficult challenge to justify a decision to sacrifice "claims of associational freedom"[53]—grounded as such in "expressive association or in intimate association"[54]—in order to protect public morality. Accordingly, care must be taken by the state to eschew administrative, judicial, or legislative determinations which abridge "choices central to personal dignity and autonomy...central to the liberty protected by the Fourteenth Amendment."[55]

It is logical to assume that the right to compassionate care in end-stage illness is, indeed, grounded in a liberty interest and, thus, cannot be unduly challenged or restricted by a state interest in judging the "morality" of autonomous actions designed to give purpose and promote dignity to the basic interest in liberty to die with dignity.[56] Society's primary obligation is to refrain from mandating one moral code over another—thus endeavoring to define and safeguard "the liberty of all"[57] and thereby promote social policies which address suffering with charity, compassion and common sense.[58] Inextricable to this societal obligation is recognition of a co-ordinate duty of healthcare providers "not to prolong dying."[59] This duty arguably coalesces with and, indeed, validates the very principle of beneficence,[60] and—accordingly—shapes a new "right" of the terminally ill not to enhance refractory pain and existential suffering at the end-stage of life.[61]

The conclusion of The New York State Task Force on Life and the Law in its 1997 supplemental report to *When Death is Sought*, serves not only as an aspirational call to action but also as a telling indictment of the tragic state of health care delivery at the end-of-life.[62]

> The widespread public interest in physician-assisted suicide represent a symptom of a much larger problem: our collective failure to respond

DOI: 10.1057/9781137377395

adequately to the suffering that patients often experience at the end of life. Improving palliative care, and attending to the psychological, spiritual, and social need of dying patients, must be a critical national priority.[63]

Growing acceptance, or even approval, of the right of the terminally ill to receive assistance in ending their lives—as is done in the United States, in the states of Oregon,[64] Washington and Vermont,[65] and in parts of Europe, notably, the Netherlands, Belgium and Switzerland[66]—should not be stymied by fear that these actions will force society, irretrievably, onto a slippery slope ending in the unequivocal endorsement and unrestricted practice of active euthanasia.[67] Rather than fear being used as an excuse for passivity or ineptitude, public policy and contemporary standards of normative conduct should be grounded in simple notions of compassionate dignity, beneficence, mercy or charity in end-stage decisionmaking.[68] This conduct will, ideally, then conduce to a simple recognition that there must be a human right to avoid intractable somatic and non-somatic pain and suffering and to be immune from cruel and unusual punishment[69] by being forced to live when futile medical conditions are present.[70]

The slippery slope is, in reality, nothing more than the human condition and, as such, "we are already on it and unable to escape it."[71] The common duty of man is to but "struggle along" in reaching a common destiny—a life struggle which is either "upwards or downwards, with very uncertain footing."[72] No safe plateau of moral security is ever reached in this journey of life."[73] Rather, painful dilemmas of choice are a given rather than the exception. Perhaps, in reality, the "goal of the human moral effort" should be simply "to keep seeing and drawing the line, and struggling to stay above it."[74]

Notes

1   Timothy E. Quill, *Physician-Assisted Death in The United States: Are the Existing 'Last Resorts' Enough?*, 38 HASTINGS CENTER RPT. 17, 21 (Sept.–Oct. 2008).

2   PRESIDENT'S COUNCIL ON BIOETHICS, TAKING CARE: ETHICAL CAREGIVING IN OUR AGING SOCIETY 217 (2005).
    See Charles Ornstein, *Deciding when to let Mom die*, WASH. POST, Mar. 3, 2013, at B1 (concluding that the standard of best possible care should not always mean keeping people alive or undertaking the most aggressive cancer chemotherapy).

DOI: 10.1057/9781137377395

See also THOMASMA and GRABER, *supra* Ch. 1, note 70 at 192 *passim*; PELLEGRINO and THOMASMA, *supra* Ch. 1, note 70 at Chs. 2, 5.

3 *See supra* notes Ch. 1, 14–20.

4 THOMASMA and GRABER, *supra* note 2 at 192.

5 *See supra* Ch. 1, notes 25–33. *See also American Medical Association, Sedation to Unconsciousness in End-of-Life Care*, CEJA RPT. 5-A-08 (2008).

6 6 6. *See* MICHAEL ROSEN, DIGNITY: ITS HISTORY AND MEANING (2012); Rex D. Glensy, *The Right to Dignity*, 43 COLUM. HUM. RTS. L. REV. 65 (2011); Death with Dignity National Center *supra* Ch. 2, note 40.

7 Pellegrino, *supra* Ch. 3, note 4.

8 *See* Ch. 3, *supra* notes 80–91 and accompanying text; Knauer, *supra* Ch. 1, note 8. *See also* Barry R. Furrow, *Pain Management and Provider Liability: No More Excuses*, 29 J. L. MED. and ETHICS 28 (2001).

9 *See e.g.,* Ch. 3, *supra* notes 7–19.

10 *See e.g.,* Ch. 3, *supra* notes 61–5.

11 *See e.g.,* Ch. 4, *supra* notes 76–82.

12 *See e.g.,* Ch. 5, *supra* notes 94–102.

13 *See e.g.,* Ch. 3, *supra* notes 80–5.

14 *See e.g.,* Ch. 1, *supra* notes 54, 67.

15 *See e.g.,* Ch. 1, *supra* note 49; Ch. 4, note 27.

16 *See e.g.,* Ch. 4, *supra* notes 89–90.
See Susan L. Mitchell et al., *The Clinical Course of Advanced Dementia*, 361 NEW ENG. J. MED. 1529, 1535 (Oct. 15, 2009).

17 GEORGE P. SMITH, II, FINAL CHOICES: AUTONOMY IN HEALTH CARE DECISIONS 109 (1989).
Indeed, a dominate concern in testing the extent to which the terminally ill patient is rational and competent to make health care decisions is the extent to which the decisions are consistent with the patient's life values. *See* WERTH, *supra* Ch. 2, note 76.

18 *Id.,* SMITH at 109.

19 WERTH, *supra* note 17.
See DAVID H. SMITH, PARTNERSHIP WITH THE DYING: WHERE MEDICINE AND MINISTRY SHOULD MEET Chs. 2, 5 (2005); *supra* Ch. 4, note 65.

20 SMITH, *supra* note 17 at 109.
See THE STUDY OF DYING: FROM AUTONOMY TO TRANSFORMATION (Allan Kellehear ed. 2009).

21 Emily Jackson, *Death, Euthanasia and The Medical Profession* in DEATH RITES AND RIGHTS, Ch. 3 at 49 (Belinda Brooks-Gordon et al., eds. 2007).

22 SMITH, *supra* note 17 at 180.

23 *See supra* Ch. 6 notes 71–6.
See PELLEGRINO and THOMASMA, *supra* note 2; Quill, Ch. 3, *supra* note 5.

DOI: 10.1057/9781137377395

24   *See* BARRY R. SCHALLER, UNDERSTANDING BIOETHICS AND
     THE LAW 4 (2008) (where "ethics" is used to describe the convergence
     of ethics and economics and recognition taken of the concern that opens
     acknowledgment of this convergence and is oftentimes avoided for fear
     that its recognition would in some way dehumanize the process of medical
     decisionmaking).
     See Boyle, Ch. 4 *supra* note 35 (discussing proportionalism as a
     consequentialist form of moral analysis where, in order to reach a moral
     judgment, all aspects of an action—including its side effects—are compared
     or balanced in terms of their ultimate effect on the human good).

25   SMITH, *supra* note 17 at 173–74.
     See Schneiderman et al., Ch. 3, *supra* note 13 (discerning the doctrine of
     medical futility as the basis of common sense).

26   CALLAHAN, *supra* Ch. 5, note 69 at 203–06.

27   *See supra* Ch. 3, notes 11–22 and accompanying text.
     For patients with advanced dementia, typical complications will include
     pneumonia, incontinence, limited verbal communication, eating difficulties
     and febrile episodes—all of which are correlated, directly, with morality rates
     of six months. These distressing symptoms should be palliated rather than
     treated aggressively and, thus, inhumanely. Mitchell et al., *supra* note 16 at
     1529; Greg A. Sachs, *Dying from Dementia*, 361 NEW ENG. J. MED. 1595, 1596
     (Oct. 15, 2009). *See* R. Sean Morrison and Albert L. Siu, *Survival in End-Stage
     Dementia Following Acute Ilness*, 284 JAMA 47 (July 5, 2000).
     For Callahan, testing the burdens and benefits of treatment modalities is
     tied ultimately to the principle of medical futility. Accordingly, when there
     is a significant likelihood that the end result of further treatment will either
     raise a strong probability of death, entail a very real probability of death
     that treatment will bring extended pain and suffering, extend a state of
     unconsciousness which is not curative or when available treatment—while
     promising an extension of life—increases greatly the near certainty of "a bad
     death," then, these forms of treatment are classified as medically futile and
     improper to undertake. CALLAHAN, *supra* note 26 at 201–02.
     See generally GEORGE P. SMITH, II, FAMILY VALUES AND THE NEW
     SOCIETY: DILEMMAS OF THE 21ST CENTURY, Ch. 8 (1998).

28   TIMOTHY E. QUILL, DEATH AND DIGNITY: MAKING CHOICES,
     AND TAKING CHARGE 51 (1994).

29   *See* MARGARET P. BATTIN, THE LEAST WORST DEATH (1994);
     JOHNSTON, *supra* note 26.

30   Graham Scambler, *Death on the Edge of the Lifeworld*, in DEATH RITES AND
     RIGHTS, Ch. 10 at 172 (Belinda Brooks-Gordon et al., eds. 2007).
     Others see a good death providing time to come to terms with one's life and
     "those with whom we have lived it—to thank and be thanked, to forgive and

DOI: 10.1057/9781137377395

be forgiven." Manuel Roig-Franzia, *The End is Near*, WASH. POST MAG. 6, 17 (quoting Rev. David Mott, Baltimore, Md.).

See GEORGE P. SMITH, II, LAW AND BIOETHICS: INTERSECTIONS ALONG THE MORTAL COIL Ch. 8 (2012); MARILYN WEBB, THE GOOD DEATH: THE NEW AMERICAN SEARCH TO RESHAPE THE END OF LIFE (1997).

31   Annas, *supra* Ch. 2, note 45 at 1102; MEISEL, *supra* Ch. 5, note 21.

A nation-wide poll of 1,500 adults released by The Pew Research Center in January, 2006, regarding American viewpoints on end-of-life care, found an overwhelming majority of the public supports laws which give patients the right to decide whether they wish to be treated medically. Some 70% of those in the survey expressed the view that there are circumstances under which they should be allowed to die. Indeed, 60% held to the belief that one has a moral right to end life if they are suffering intractable pain and have no hope of improvement or, in other words, is in a futile medical state and/or suffering from an incurable disease. Pew Center Press Release, *supra* Ch. 1 at note 49.

32   *See* New York Task Force Report, 1997 Supplement, *supra* Ch. 5, note 1 at 5. *See also* SHEPHERD, Ch. 4, *supra* note 79 at Ch. 7; Moncreif, *supra* Ch. 1, note 24 at 2217–23.

With the legalization of assisted suicide, Judge Richard Posner asserts— based on empirical reasoning and a utilitarian calculus—that such action could lead to fewer, rather than more, suicides. The argument advanced here is that those overwhelmed with the fear of becoming totally incapacitated from terminal medical conditions are forced into a course of action which means that they either kill themselves while still capable, or, face the distinct prospect of ultimately becoming incompetent and losing their autonomy to act accordingly. Whether such a course of action would be cost-effective remains difficult to determine, however, since the medical costs associated with administering this assistance could be borne by the public. RICHARD A. POSNER, AGING AND OLD AGE 243–51 (1995).

33   Patient Self-Determination Act, 42 U.S.C. §§1395 cc(f) (Medicare), 1396 a(a) (Medicaid) (1994).

See supra Ch. 3, notes 39–42 and accompanying text.

34   *See* Ulrich, *supra* Ch. 3, note 40.

35   *Id.*

But see Rebecca Dresser, *Precommitment: A Misguided Strategy for Securing Death with Dignity*, 81 TEX. L. REV. 1823 (2003) (questioning the relevance of advance treatment choices as misguided and morally troubling and often in conflict with a physician's responsibility to protect incompetent patients from harm).

36   *See supra* Ch. 3, notes 22, 59–65 and accompanying text.

DOI: 10.1057/9781137377395

37   *See supra* Ch. 5, note 36.
38   OREGON REV. STAT. §§127.800 (12), 127.805 (2005).
39   VT. STAT. ANN. Ch. 113, §5281 (2013); REV. CODE WASH. ANN., Ch. 70,245 (2009).
40   *See e.g., supra* Ch. 4 notes 78–84 for the suggestions of the American Academy of Palliative Medicine; *supra* Ch. 3, notes 94–110, for the suggestions of the American Medical Association.
41   *See* Smith *supra* Ch. 2, note 47.
     See JONATHAN BARON, AGAINST BIOETHICS Ch. 3 (2006) (stressing the ineluctable foundation of utilitarianism as the preferred basis for bioethical decisionmaking).
42   *See generally* Vijay N. Joish and Gary M. Oderda, *Cost Utility Analysis of Quality Adjusted Years*, 19 J. PAIN & PALLIATIVE CARE PHARMACOTHERAPY 57 (2005).
     It has been suggested that any determination of futility must be a joint determination made, as such, by physician, patient and surrogate decision maker, with the final determination endeavoring to strike a balance between three criteria: effectiveness, benefit, and burden—in achieving the patient's good. Pellegrino, *supra* note 7 at 227.
43   Pellegrino, *supra* note 7 at 220, 227.
     See generally Amir Halevy, *Medical Futility, Patient Autonomy, and Professional Integrity: Finding the Appropriate Balance*, 18 HEALTH MATRIX 261 (2008).
44   Defined as a sense of Christian love, charity. I OXFORD ENGLISH DICTIONARY 243 (2nd ed. 1998).
45   Defined as Christian love. III OXFORD ENGLISH DICTIONARY 42 (2nd ed. 1998).
     See Pellegrino, *supra* Ch. 3, note 4 at 241 (where charity is advanced as an attribute of end-of-life care and treatment).
46   Defined as pity. III OXFORD ENGLISH DICTIONARY 597 (2nd ed. 1998).
47   Defined as benevolence. IV OXFORD ENGLISH DICTIONARY 52 (2nd ed. 1998).
     See Fletcher, *supra* Ch. 2 note 54.
48   Defined as mercy, showing compassion or kindness. IX OXFORD ENGLISH DICTIONARY 626 (2nd ed. 1998).
49   POSNER, *supra* Ch. 6, note 39 at 116. *Emphasis added.*
     See Schneiderman et al., *supra* Ch. 3, note 13 at 409 (regarding the basis of common sense).
50   Pellegrino, *supra* Ch. 3, note 4 at 233–35.
51   *Id.* at 223.
     See e.g., the "Locked-in Syndrome" British case of Tony Nicklinson, Ch. 2, *supra* note 56.
     See generally PELLEGRINO and THOMASMA, *supra* note 2.

DOI: 10.1057/9781137377395

52 Laurence H. Tribe, Lawrence v. Texas: *The Fundamental Right That Dare Not Speak Its Name*, 117 HARV. L. REV. 1893, 1935–36 (2004).

53 *Id.* at 1936.

54 *Id.*

55 Planned Parenthood of Southeastern Pa. v. Case, 505 U.S. 833, 851 (1992). (Stevens, J.).

56 *See* Lawrence v. Texas, 539 U.S. 558, 573, 578 (2003).
With death control, which is a matter of human dignity, "persons become puppets." Joseph Fletcher, *Four Indicators of Humanhood—The Enquiry Matures*, 4 HASTINGS CENTER RPT. 7 (1974).
See generally RAPHAEL COHEN-ALMAGOR, THE RIGHT TO DIE WITH DIGNITY (2001); Roger F. Friedman, *It's My Body and I'll Die if I Want To: A Property-Based Argument in Support of Assisted Suicide*, 12 J. CONTEMP. HEALTH L. & POL'Y 183 (1995).

57 Planned Parenthood of Southeastern Pa. v. Casey, 505 U.S. at 850.
The right of privacy from governmental intrusions, expressed in Griswold and Eisenstadt, add to the strength of the liberty of associational expression found in Lawrence, in arguing for a right to die with dignity without unduly burdensome state interference.
See Griswold v. Connecticut, 381 U.S. 479 (1965); Eisenstadt v. Baird, 405 U.S. 438 (1972).

58 THOMASMA, *supra* Ch. 1, note 70 at 195.
See George P. Smith, II, *Managing Death: End of Life Charades and Decisions*, Ch. 6 in AGING DECISIONS AT THE END OF LIFE (David N. Weisstub et al., eds. 2001).

59 THOMASMA, *id.*
This duty should be triggered when one is diagnosed as terminally ill, has made a determination (or executed an advance directive) that, because of medical conditions, life no longer has persona meaning or, when, even though no such decision has been made by the patient and there is no advance directive, there is nonetheless a medical realization that the terminal illness is "in its imminent phase." THOMASMA, *id.* at 194.

60 PELLEGRINO and THOMASMA, *supra* note 2.

61 *See* CASSELL, *supra* Ch. 2, note 6.
See also Berger, *supra* Ch. 2, note 75.

62 *Supra* Ch. 5, note 1, New York State Task Force, 1997 Supplemental Report.

63 *Id.* at 12.

64 ORE. REV. STAT. §§ 127.800 (12), 127.805 (2005).

65 REV. CODE WASH. ANN., Ch. 70, 245 (2009).
18 VT. STAT. ANN. Ch. 113, §5281 (2013).

66 GRIFFITHS et al., *supra* Ch. 2, note 59; HUMPHRY, *supra* Ch. 2, note 40; Zweymert, *supra* Ch. 2, note 66 (noting the unsuccessful efforts of Baron Joel

Joffe to enact legislation in Britain comparable to the Oregon law allowing medical assistance for the terminally ill); Len Doyal, *supra* Ch. 5, note 1.

67   *See generally* George P. Smith, II, MONOGRAPH, *Euthanasia, Suicide or Self-Determination—Ethical, Legal and Philosophical Concerns* (1999).

68   *Supra* notes 22–3, 43–8, 56, 58, 60.
      See CHARLES FOSTER, CHOOSING LIFE, CHOOSING DEATH, Chs. 2, 11 (2009).

69   *See generally* Smith, MONOGRAPH, *supra* Ch. 2, note 45.

70   Smith, *All's Well That Ends Well, supra* Ch. 2, note 34.
      Finding a moral similarity between physician-assisted suicide and active euthanasia, it has been argued that fairness requires that if physician-assisted death is recognized legally, recognition must also be given to a variant of active euthanasia which allows a patient—unable physically to commit physician-assisted death or wishing to end his life by lethal injection but unable to self administer—to rely upon, legally, an attending physician to act accordingly to end his suffering. Nicholas Dixon, *On The Difference between Physician-Assisted Suicide and Active Euthanasia* 28 HASTINGS CENTER RPT. 25 (1998).

      See Len Doyal, *supra* Ch 2, note 24 arguing that autonomy should be de-emphasized as the operative principle in decisionmaking and, instead, a standard of common dignity, mercy or best interests of the dying should be controlling. Accordingly, since competent patients suffering from a terminal illness can choose to refuse treatment, why "should it not be possible for clinicians, in partnership with families, to make similar decisions on behalf of those who cannot competently choose for themselves." *Id.*

      THOMASMA and GRABER stress the notion that there should be a communitarian or societal obligation to relieve pain and suffering which exceeds the individual right to forego such. *Supra* note 2 at 193.

71   George P. Smith, II, MONOGRAPH, When Mercy Seasons Justice 21 (2007).

72   *Id.* at 21, n. 101 citing Minette Marrian, *An Acceptable Way to Arrange our Death*, http://www.timesonline.co.uk/article/0.2088-2179494.00.

73   Marrian, *id.*
      Instead of being a rush toward moral oblivion, recognition of assisted dying may well "be a step uphill to a better society" where a greater opportunity for deeper moral development occurs and—consequently—fosters a more compassionate understanding of the end-stage of life. CHARLES F. McKHANN, A TIME TO DIE: THE PLACE OF PHYSICIAN ASSISTANCE 239, 240 (1999).

74   Marrian, *id.*

DOI: 10.1057/9781137377395

Select Bibliography

Margaret P. Battin, ENDING LIFE. New York: Oxford University Press, 2005.

Margaret P. Battin, THE LEAST WORST DEATH. New York: Oxford University Press, 1994.

Daniel Callahan, THE TROUBLED DREAM OF LIFE. Washington, DC: Georgetown University Press, 2000.

John Fletcher, SITUATION ETHICS. Louisville, KY: Westminster John Knox Press, 1966.

Charles Foster, CHOOSING LIFE, CHOOSING DEATH. Oxford: Hart Publishing Company, 2009.

Jonathan Herring, CARING AND THE LAW. Oxford: Hart Publishing Company, 2013.

Shai J. Lavi, THE MODERN ART OF DYING. Princeton, NJ: Princeton University Press, 2005.

Guenther Lewy, ASSISTED DEATH IN EUROPE AND AMERICA. New York: Oxford University Press, 2011.

Roger Magnusson, ANGELS OF DEATH. New Haven: Yale University Press, 2002.

Margaret Otlowski, VOLUNTARY EUTHANASIA AND THE COMMON LAW. New York: Oxford University Press, 1997.

Edmund D. Pellegrino and David C. Thomasma, FOR THE PATIENT'S GOOD. New York: Oxford University Press, 1988.

Richard A. Posner, AGING AND OLD AGE. Chicago: University of Chicago Press, 1995.

Timothy E. Quill, DEATH AND DIGNITY, New York: W. W. Norton, 1994.

DOI: 10.1057/9781137377395

Fiona Randall and Robin S. Downie, PALLIATIVE CARE ETHICS. New York: Oxford University Press, 1996.

Lois L. Shepherd, IF THAT EVER HAPPENED TO ME. Chapel Hill, NC: University of North Carolina Press, 2009.

David C. Thomasma, HUMAN LIFE IN THE BALANCE. Louisville, KY: Westminster John Knox Press, 1990.

David C. Thomasma and Glen C. Graber, EUTHANASIA. New York: Continuum, 1991.

Robert Young, MEDICALLY ASSISTED DEATH. Cambridge: Cambridge University Press, 2007.

DOI: 10.1057/9781137377395

Index

DOI: 10.1057/9781137377395

9 781137 379153